John Steinbeck and the Critics

This work by a prominent Steinbeck scholar begins with a study of the novelist's early celebrity in the 1930s and 1940s. Professor Ditsky shows that by the late 1940s there is some falling off in Steinbeck's critical reputation, and yet that is also the period in which the "first generation" of Steinbeck critics did their first work: seminal commentary by Peter Lisca, Warren French, and Joseph Fontenrose. These critics were unwilling to accept the fact that the proletarian writer of the 1930s was a thing of the past, and that formally he had become much more experimental. In the 1960s, a second generation of critics such as Robert DeMott, Louis Owens, Mimi Gladstein and others, led by the Steinbeck Society's Tetsumaro Hayashi, began to show, if hardly adoringly, what the later Steinbeck was about. As the anniversaries of publication of the classic early works approached in the 1970s, there was a quantitative peaking of book-length criticism, accompanied by a spate of conferences in various worldwide venues. A number of anthologies of journal-published articles were published, including one edited by Professor Ditsky. The last two decades have seen new voices emerge, many going beyond close readings to apply contemporary critical methods to a writer increasingly seen as postmodernist.

John Ditsky teaches creative writing at the University of Windsor, Ontario, Canada. He has published more than 1300 poems, and has written four critical works, three of them on Steinbeck.

Studies in American Literature and Culture:
Literary Criticism in Perspective

Editorial Board

Literary Criticism in Perspective

James Hardin (*South Carolina*), General Editor

Stephen D. Dowden (*Brandeis*), German Literature

About *Literary Criticism in Perspective*

Books in the series *Literary Criticism in Perspective* trace literary scholarship and criticism on major and neglected writers alike, or on a single major work, a group of writers, a literary school or movement. In so doing the authors — authorities on the topic in question who are also well-versed in the principles and history of literary criticism — address a readership consisting of scholars, students of literature at the graduate and undergraduate level, and the general reader. One of the primary purposes of the series is to illuminate the nature of literary criticism itself, to gauge the influence of social and historic currents on aesthetic judgments once thought objective and normative.

JOHN DITSKY

JOHN STEINBECK
AND THE CRITICS

CAMDEN HOUSE

First published 2000
by Camden House

Camden House is an imprint of Boydell & Brewer Inc.
PO Box 41026, Rochester, NY 14604–4126 USA
and of Boydell & Brewer Limited
PO Box 9, Woodbridge, Suffolk IP12 3DF, UK

ISBN: 1–57113–210–4

Library of Congress Cataloging-in-Publication Data

Ditsky, John.
    John Steinbeck and the critics / John Ditsky.
        p. cm. – (Studies in American literature and culture. Literary criticism
    in perspective)
    Includes bibliographical references and index.
    ISBN 1–57113–210–4 (alk. paper)
    1. Steinbeck, John, 1902–1968—Criticism and interpretation—History. 2.
    Criticism—United States—History—20th century. I. Title. II. Series.

    PS3537.T3234 Z6278 2000
    813'.52—dc21
                                                                    00–036104

A catalogue record for this title is available from the British Library.

This publication is printed on acid-free paper.
Printed in the United States of America

To my late mother, who taught me to read,
and father, who taught me to work, and of course
to my most patient wife Sue, who has put up with
the tantrums that result when the effects
of reading and working intermix in too heady
and unstable an emulsion. And to daughter Kate,
who is always teaching us something.

Contents

Acknowledgments

ANYTHING BUT A SHORT LIST would be unfair to the many people who have helped and influenced me through the years, but I would especially mention Tetsumaro Hayashi, whose relentless zeal drove many of us onward for a quarter of a century, Roy S. Simmonds, who has been a faithful and most encouraging correspondent for well over a decade, and Robert DeMott, the most impressive and thorough scholar of Steinbeck in our generation, and an excellent friend. I could not have completed this manuscript without the consistent and caring attention of Lorraine Cantin, who word-processed it — over and over again. Finally, I must thank my University of Windsor and its plucky Department of English for this final sabbatical time and for the unique opportunity for this American to teach John Steinbeck to his heart's delight on soil hardly foreign.

Introduction

L IKE OTHER VOLUMES IN THE SERIES *Literary Criticism in Perspective*, this one on John Steinbeck (1902–68) attempts to give the reader an idea of the shape and direction of Steinbeck criticism over the past sixty years. That criticism has been fairly voluminous, of late increasingly so; and thus it has been necessary to confine this survey to critical books. However, many of the best critical articles on Steinbeck's work have been gathered in the book-length collections covered herein. It has also been necessary to exclude critical surveys in which John Steinbeck plays only a nominal role.

However, the flexibility which marks this series apart from its lock-step predecessors meant that I was able to include mention of all books written on Steinbeck to date, with proportionate attention awarded according to worth — or its felt lack. There have been bibliographies and bibliographical studies of Steinbeck criticism before this one, but none has been allowed the scope of coverage this full-length survey offers, and of course none is as up-to-date. Rather than mention these earlier efforts here, then, they will be covered in their appropriate niches in the five chapters to come.

I have attempted to provide a sense of the development of Steinbeck criticism in book form in these chapters, and my presentation is therefore almost wholly chronological. The exception is to be found in the third chapter, in which the efforts of Tetsumaro Hayashi and the Steinbeck Society, which cover three decades of serious attention and catalytic enterprise, are shown as reflecting in themselves the major changes in direction of Steinbeck criticism in its most crucial years.

Thus I hope I have been able to satisfy the norms on which this series was founded while taking advantage of the freedom it offered me to present a fuller, more comprehensive coverage.

Excluded for reasons of relative unavailability are books published in countries other than the United States, Canada, and the United Kingdom. This is regrettable but necessary, since Steinbeck has been widely translated throughout the world, and even though the Asian contingent of the International John Steinbeck Society, especially the Japanese membership, has been considerably active in Steinbeck studies — and in organizing the International Steinbeck Congresses, which are held every five years or so and will likely see a fifth occurrence on the centenary of Steinbeck's birth in 2002. Also excluded are study guides meant only for younger readers, most field guides to Steinbeck country, and the like, that is, books meant for the tourist and the novice. Our intended readership consists of serious university students, both undergraduate and graduate; professional scholars; educated lay readers, bibliophiles, and librarians. But purely bibliographical studies have also had to be excluded, that is, those meant for collectors of particular editions or those interested in collection holdings; those titles of interest to general Steinbeck scholars have been dealt with in turn. In addition, special Steinbeck numbers of various literary journals have also been omitted owing to difficulty of acquisition.

Additionally, there has not been either space or rationale to include the new, larger-format Penguin editions of Steinbeck titles, an ongoing series with (to date) uniformly excellent introductions — but only introductions.

As for obtaining personal, professional, or institutional copies of the titles surveyed herein, the news is quite good. A number of dealers, particularly in California, offer Steinbeck titles as specialty items. Moreover, as work on Steinbeck has increasingly moved from token offerings from major commercial publishing houses to series titles from smaller presses living off sales to libraries, and (as Steinbeck's reputation has been buttressed by further fresh critical activity) to the university presses — which are much more likely to maintain a serious backlist over time — these books are mostly out there for the obtaining, especially with the help of the Internet. Good hunting! I hope I have succeeded at my task.

1: Pioneers

THOUGH JOHN STEINBECK'S FIRST NOVEL, *Cup of Gold*, was published as early as 1929, it was not until well after *The Pastures of Heaven* (1932), *To a God Unknown* (1933), *Tortilla Flat* (1935*)*, *In Dubious Battle* (1936), and even *Of Mice and Men* (1937) and *The Long Valley* (1938) that Harry Thornton Moore's *The Novels of John Steinbeck: A First Study* appeared, that is, in the year in which the world received his acknowledged masterpiece *The Grapes of Wrath* (1939).

We might well wonder why it took a decade to begin to give Steinbeck serious critical attention at book length. The defensive Steinbeckians of years ago might have been quick to point to the palpable bias of East Coast intellectuals against writers from the West or, for that matter, the South and even the Midwest. The point is by now largely moot. The fact remains that Steinbeck, with *Grapes*, had written a mighty book with a mighty theme, as Melville would have put it, and by encapsulating a major development in American history, the westward migration of victims of the 1930s Dust Bowl conditions, he could no longer be ignored.

For John Steinbeck understood that the thirties had rekindled the pioneer spirit among Americans who had only, as it were, paused in their westward trek almost half a century earlier. Whether they understood this consciously we cannot know, but that John Steinbeck understood their most instinctive perceptions we cannot doubt. It is interesting that this first study should have included what has become a standard feature in critical volumes on Steinbeck: the area map. Maps and charts based on "Steinbeck country" have been a feature of Steinbeck criticism from the beginning, usually indicating the "real" or putative locales where his fictions are based. Implications of such "facts" are not wholly innocent, nor are they a matter of informing ignorant easterners about the territory they are reading about, perhaps for the first time. For the identification of Steinbeck with northern California south of San Francisco had a considerable impact on the first decades of Steinbeck criticism; it is surely part of why his first important critics could not stomach his moves to other locales, such as Europe and the East. Steinbeck's abandoning of his native region surely played a role in tempting his early major critics to conclude that in the process, he betrayed not only his roots and his philosophy, but also his art.

In fairness to Steinbeck, it is accurate to note that some of his critics could not accommodate his growth as an artist. The fellow whom such critics grew up admiring in their early careers refused to avoid change, and while he changed into something of a postmodernist, they continued to cherish the quondam socialist. But it is not the purpose of this project to evaluate this difference of opinion.

It remains something of a mystery that, given the power of Steinbeck's first publications and their regional concerns and relevancies — the pirate potboiler *Cup of Gold* of course excluded — it took longer until the West was awake to him. And even a casual (but educated) reader of *Cup* should have been alerted to the fact that Steinbeck was mesmerized by Arthurian themes and devices; such a reader should also have been able to pursue that notion through succeeding works wherein main characters, generally male, bond (if only fitfully) in quest of some elusive ideal, usually epitomized as female, some holy "cup," in other words, some grail.

Considering the fact that Moore's *The Novels of John Steinbeck* is the first volume of its kind, the book holds up well even today. Its observations are judicious, such as when Moore observes of *Cup of Gold* that its young author "had not yet reached the stage where he could bring all his people fully to life" (Moore 15), whereas *The Pastures of Heaven* contains "imaginative touches foretelling some of Steinbeck's greatest achievements (18).

At the same time, Moore wrote too soon after the publication of *The Grapes of Wrath* to have fully come to terms with it. He repeats the mistaken assumption that Steinbeck traveled west with the Okies (88). He places Steinbeck with Thomas Wolfe among novelists who attempt to combine the individual and the universal, noting that the "only American who has successfully created life-in-literature on the scale of the great writers of the earth is Herman Melville," seemingly brushing off a certain Mississippian contemporary of both Wolfe and Steinbeck; and not all readers of *Grapes* would agree that in the end the book lacks "well proportioned and intensified drama," or that "[t]here is no vital conflict in *The Grapes of Wrath*" (68–69). However, Moore senses Steinbeck's ambitious tackling of issues of scale, and it is in those terms that he finds the novel to have fallen short. In the end, it is too bad that we do not have the chance to see what Harry Thornton Moore might have said about the next two decades of Steinbeck's fiction.

In particular, Moore very pertinently raises the issue of *place* in a way that is prescient, that is, prophetic of studies yet to come:

> In every discussion of a Steinbeck story a good deal of space may safely be devoted to examining the author's power of evoking that quality we have no satisfactory word for — it is what the Germans call *"Stimmung,"* and what we try to try to approximate with the word "atmosphere." Steinbeck is perhaps more interested than any writer since D. H. Lawrence in what Lawrence called the Spirit of Place. But this is only the lyric side of novel-writing. Steinbeck . . . has worked within the established borders of novel-writing, so we may fairly use the customary methods of judgment when scrutinizing his characters and their problems. (15)

In other words, Moore seemed — in 1939 — to be open to the notion of thematic portability. Moore, unlike his later colleagues, might have allowed Steinbeck more room to grow.

In the same year as Moore's critical volume, 1939, there also appeared a brochure entitled *John Steinbeck: Personal and Bibliographical Notes,* written by newspaper reviewer Lewis Gannett. This brief work is of little worth to today's reader, and not merely because it (unlike Moore's volume) consists almost wholly of anecdotal information, but on the grounds that it is essentially an attempt to sell titles from the Steinbeck list of Viking Press, which had acquired publication rights to Steinbeck's earliest titles in 1938 and intended to print everything he would write from then on. Consider the differences between Gannett's conclusion and Moore's: Gannett writes of Steinbeck's decision to write the "saga" of the Okies, "It took him a long time, and it made his biggest and richest and ripest, his toughest book and his tenderest, *The Grapes of Wrath"* (Gannett, *Notes* 14). Even readers inclined to agree will recognize puffery when they see it; the work is essentially a long jacket blurb.

Gannett continued to be useful to Viking and Steinbeck when in 1943 he compiled *The Portable Steinbeck,* one of the very first titles in that extremely popular series. The anthology was a sign of Steinbeck's sustained ability to sell books and please his readers, and it contained the full texts of *The Red Pony* and *Of Mice and Men,* along with substantial excerpts from the best of Steinbeck's other novels and stories. Reflecting the times, a fair amount of war-related material was included, and that amount increased when the volume was revised in 1946. (The bibliographical information included continued to be updated well into the 1950s.) Gannett's contribution is again anecdotal, for the most part, although his introduction, "Steinbeck's Way of Writing," is of genuine critical interest as well as entertaining.

Towards the end of his introduction, Gannett attempts to summarize a career only halfway over:

> So there . . . is the story of a creative writer at work. Certain patterns are recurrent: the restless wandering, when a story is in gestation; the false starts; the utter absorption in creation, when the letters become sparser and the work is everything; finally, fatigue, uncertainty of the product, and a few wisps of anger at critics' misunderstanding. The war interrupts, but merely interrupts, the recurrent pattern; and now the war is over. The rest of the autobiography is for John Steinbeck . . . to write, and it would be presumptuous for a critic to attempt to anticipate it. . . . (Gannett, *Portable* xxvii-xxviii)

This is not only a sound assessment of a pattern but a prescient adumbration of things to come. In sum, this collection in its two editions surely deserved its sales figures, and probably led many a student (and other reader) into the world of John Steinbeck.

Steinbeck had been changing some of his attitudes towards life and literature since as early, it can be argued, as *The Grapes of Wrath*. Those critics who praised his work of the 1930s because they thought him a naturalist, a proletarian, or even a communist seemed baffled, even betrayed, once they began to perceive changes in his fiction, even if they did not understand those changes. Somewhat paradoxically, this led to the first flourishing of book-length Steinbeck criticism during the late 1950s and early 1960s, when Steinbeck had largely finished his work as a writer. Whether or not they agreed on what they perceived to be going on in Steinbeck's career, a new generation of Steinbeck critics had emerged, and lively controversies over the man's merits as a writer filled the pages of a clutch of highly significant and influential critical volumes.

But first, a kind of summing up took place. In 1957, two University of New Mexico professors, E. W. Tedlock, Jr., and C. V. Wicker, published the first book collection of criticism by many hands, older work as well as new, on John Steinbeck. Called *Steinbeck and His Critics: A Record of Twenty-Five Years*, it accurately mirrors the state of Steinbeck studies from their earliest beginnings to about 1956. Though the critical-anthology approach of Tedlock and Wicker is different from the one chosen for this title, our title pays homage to theirs.

Moreover, there are six short contributions by Steinbeck himself, who had been stung years before by the critical failure of his final "play-novella," *Burning Bright*. Whether the critics did not understand what

Steinbeck was trying to do or understood it all too well is still perhaps a moot point, but it is clear from Steinbeck's essays (and letters) that the writer at first rankled under criticism, then seemed to agree that the work deserved to fail, and finally became defensive again about how critics, as opposed to creative artists, went about their work.

Hence the tone of Steinbeck's reprinted essay, "Critics, Critics, Burning Bright," together with the extra spin that Tedlock and Wicker's title gives the word. It must be noted that the book's editors appear to agree with the writer for their own prudent reasons, reflecting shared attitudes in an era when the close readings of a generation of scholars weaned on the New Criticism ran afoul of other academics who brought philosophy, along with notions of what a writer is allowed to do, to their commentaries. Such a defense of what Steinbeck chose to do on behalf of his art is appropriate to not only the time but the writer himself, whose works appear to invite surface readings because of their approachability.

Thus it is highly ironic that at the end of their thorough introduction to their volume, in which they have dealt in depth with the contents and approaches of the critics included, Tedlock and Wicker compare their experience as critical anthologists to coming home from a cocktail party "late at night not entirely sure what all the talk was about but determined to think about it some other and soberer day" (Tedlock and Wicker xl). The irony lies in the fact that in the process of making their call for fairness in reading Steinbeck, they almost precisely reverse the reasoning of today's new students of Steinbeck (yet to be heard from in this volume), who argue that we need new ways to read the man, and that inevitably means bringing critical theory into play.

Tedlock and Wicker conclude that "many of the reviewers and critics have made serious blunders," and we presume they include in the statement even their own choices, especially "when they deal with his so-called philosophy":

> They start with assumptions of what a correct philosophy is and judge Steinbeck's fiction to be faulty because he does not agree with them. They show themselves unable or unwilling to follow the old, sane, fundamental rule which obligates critics to try to understand the author's intention and to judge his success or failure in realizing it before they shift ground to more universal and . . . controversial considerations. . . . there is a tendency to call him a realist and then to condemn him because he is not the critic's particular brand of realist . . . despite the fact that even in his early work it ought to have been apparent that Steinbeck characteristically worked through sym-

bol and myth as well as some sort of verisimilitude and that to read him on only one level, that of mere story, was to miss the point. (xl)

Similarly, the editors deal with the charge against Steinbeck of sentimentality, noting that there is "nothing disreputable about combining in a single vision of life an objective attitude and affection" (xli).

The critical common sense expressed by the editors above does not prevent them from suggesting that some of Steinbeck's "attitudes towards critics, and intellectuals in general . . . show an antagonism more suited to the Bohemian rebellions of the Twenties than to the responsibility-demanding Fifties" (xli). One wonders what Steinbeck would have made of the editors' allusion to the "responsibility-demanding Fifties," since a few years later he would be publishing his last novel, *The Winter of Our Discontent*, which took a vastly different attitude towards the 1950s and notions of personal duty. Unless Tedlock and Wicker were especially far-sighted, it is likely that Steinbeck did not find that responsibility was really demanded, as it were, until the 1961 Inauguration of President Kennedy, since he regretted deeply his country's double rejection of the candidacy of Adlai E. Stevenson.

With this speculation I mean to place in temporal context Tedlock and Wicker's choices for inclusion, especially the earliest. Some of the writers appear twice, and their contributions are staples of the Steinbeck critical canon. These include Joseph Warren Beach's "John Steinbeck: Journeyman Artist" and "John Steinbeck: Art and Propaganda," Frederic I. Carpenter's "John Steinbeck: American Dreamer" and "The Philosophical Joads" (with its famous tracing of Steinbeck's ideas to American thinkers of the middle and late nineteenth century); Woodburn O. Ross's "John Steinbeck: Earth and Stars" and "John Steinbeck: Naturalism's Priest"; and Martin Staples Shockley's "The Reception of *The Grapes of Wrath* in Oklahoma." Other essays have proved lastingly challenging over the years. The salient point here, where individual essays cannot be given much space, is that the editors made excellent choices that do more than fix Steinbeck criticism in a time venue a decade before the writer's death: They also eerily predict the course of future Steinbeck criticism.

The state of uncertainty Steinbeck had been arousing among his critics for more than a decade is apparent in the anthology's last entry by one of them, Joseph Wood Krutch who, in *The New York Herald Tribune Book Review*, reviewed *East of Eden* and was chastened into cautiousness by the implications of his task. Krutch does his best not to be precipitously judgmental about what he has noted:

Moral relativism and some sort of deterministic philosophy have commonly seemed to be implied in the writings of that school of hard-boiled realists with which Mr. Steinbeck has sometimes been loosely associated. It is difficult to imagine how any novel could more explicitly reject both than they are rejected in "East of Eden." The author, who was acclaimed as a social critic in "The Grapes of Wrath" and sometimes abused as a mere writer of sensational melodrama in some subsequent books, plainly announces here that it is as a moralist that he wants to be taken. (305)

And then Krutch simultaneously waffles about his stance on this perceived change in Steinbeck's strategy and puts his finger on the new issue not yet ready to be settled:

The merits of so ambitious and absorbing a book are sure to be widely and hotly debated. The final verdict will not, I think, depend upon the validity of the thesis which is part of a debate almost as old as human thought or upon any possible doubt concerning the vividness of Mr. Steinbeck's storytelling. On the highest level the question is this: Does the fable really carry the thesis; is the moral implicit in or merely imposed upon the story; has the author recreated a myth or merely moralized a tale? There is no question that Mr. Steinbeck has written an intensely interesting and impressive book. (305)

Not at all a bad response on first acquaintance.

An odd coincidence, if that, partially explains the special virtue of this volume. The editors had decided to include Lewis Gannett's *Portable Steinbeck* introduction, perhaps because Viking had decided another edition was needed and the essay was no longer profitable; in any event, Gannett's essay was accompanied by another specifically designed to be biographical but not to intrude on Gannett's established space. The writer was Peter Lisca, a doctoral student at the University of Wisconsin; and he not only wrote the new biographical material but revised sections of his doctoral dissertation on Steinbeck, on *The Wayward Bus* and *The Pearl*, specifically for this volume, and in the process managed to set the tone for the arrival of the second generation of Steinbeck critics.

And among these critics he was the first with a serious academic stake in what happened to Steinbeck studies in the next few years. With the arrival of Peter Lisca, the days when John Steinbeck was at the mercy of newspaper and magazine critics had ended. Now he was either the darling or the damned of the academics, since magazines like *Time* never pretended to like, or even to have read, his work. This in a sense made Steinbeck "respectable," since he was no longer at the very untender mercies of the purely media critics who had for so long simply badgered him.

Lisca subtitles the introduction to his 1958 publication of his dissertation, *The Wide World of John Steinbeck*, "The Failure of Criticism," leaving no doubt about his perspective. By the same token, the title of the book itself indicates that there is far more to John Steinbeck than prior critics had seen. Lisca rightly exempts Harry Thornton Moore, though he properly notes that Moore's serious and fair-minded study could of necessity deal with only half or so of Steinbeck's output and at any rate did not influence subsequent critics into more positive ways (Lisca, *Wide World* 5–6).

Lisca also states that in the decade preceding his study, only two articles on Steinbeck had appeared, both dealing with *Grapes* (18); obviously, it was time for a more comprehensive and objective venture, even if it meant taking on some of the big names who had largely deprecated and willfully misunderstood Steinbeck such as the sneering Maxwell Geismar and Frederick J. Hoffman, too, both of whom had suggested that when Steinbeck achieved a noteworthy effect, it was likely to have been an unwitting accident (19–20).

This increasingly dismissive attitude towards Steinbeck's artistry, Lisca says, can be traced to the fact that his three major successes of the 1930s, arriving at the end of the Depression and "dealing with proletarian materials," inevitably were "both accepted and rejected on sociological rather than aesthetic terms" (3). As Lisca's study makes clear, this bullheaded critical insistence on keeping Steinbeck in a box not of his making resulted in decades of distorted readings and dismissals.

In truth, Lisca and other newer critics did initially tend to put Steinbeck into a box of his own making, but the author eventually freed himself. Lisca lucidly presents the quasi-scientific ideas that influenced the early Steinbeck during his close association with marine biologist Edward F. Ricketts, the notions of a "group man" and "'is'-thinking." (The "group man" refers to the capacity to act as a species or part of a species when necessary, similar to when minnows or sparrows act in seeming unison, or geese migrate, having somehow created a leader goose at the head of a V in flight. "'Is'-thinking" means acceptance of things as they are without taking on the responsibility as scientist or artist of changing them towards what "should" be, which in turn implies the acceptance of the metaphysical imperative of what, in fiction, is the compulsory "happy ending" — surely the *true* sentimentality, as opposed to the sort Steinbeck was frequently accused of.) There are misperceptions of a writer's work, to be sure, but also nostalgic unwill-ingnesses to see one change.

Lisca's chronological survey necessarily ends prematurely with such often dismissed satirical pieces as 1957's *The Short Reign of Pippin IV;* for John Steinbeck was still writing, and Lisca could not have foreseen the relevance of *Pippin* to the later *The Winter of Our Discontent* (and the nonfiction *America and Americans*). Lisca almost casually refers, as some later critics would not, to "Steinbeck's success in fleshing out this parable to the dimensions of a credible, forceful human adventure," something he attributes to a "prose style" that is "flexible to the extent that here as in most of his other novels it becomes technique as well as medium" (225). Similarly, he praises *The Wayward Bus's* "energy" that "derives from this tension between the plot on the level of character and the plot on the level of journey" (246):

> In *The Wayward Bus* Steinbeck reveals himself at a point of stasis between the rejections of *Cannery Row* and *The Pearl* and the af-firmations of *Burning Bright* and *East of Eden.* (247)

But here Lisca, like many a Steinbeck critic before or after him, seems to have chosen as standard Steinbeck works that were written before he himself came onto the scene as a critic: his Steinbeck-nurturing, or in-culcation if you will, cannot abide very much change in authorial habits. He regards subsequent works as evidence of a "rapid decline" (228).

Thus Lisca is harsh about *Sweet Thursday* and *The Short Reign of Pippin IV,* which would have made for an unhappy era to have ended any survey of Steinbeck's career. There is now a vocabulary to describe Steinbeck's authorial adventures in these works and those that followed, but such a vocabulary was not available to Lisca at the end of the 1950s. The first generation of Steinbeck critics arrived on the scene when the writer was still practicing his art; they considered whatever came before highly worthwhile, and what came after a disappointment. Members of the second generation, including the present writer, were introduced to Steinbeck through *Grapes* in the 1950s and then worked their way backwards from *The Winter of Our Discontent* and *East of Eden* as the most proximate choices for next "reads," completely un-aware that somewhere in the 1940s there was supposed to be some moment when Steinbeck as an author "declined." Those who were slightly older opted for such a date as having come about in the early 1940s; some who came later noted no such date at all.

And so Lisca breaks ranks with Steinbeck over *East of Eden,* arguing honestly enough that "The moral philosophy of the narrator is no more convincing than its structural function, and at times seems in direct variance with the action" (267). But it never seems to have entered Lisca's consciousness that Steinbeck might have been about a new kind of fiction, one more like a cooking show on television where eggs are cracked and mistakes made before a "live" audience. He falls into the sand trap of consigning the later Steinbeck to a character, and identity, who had erred by moving from "his 'long valley' of California to the fashionable East Side of New York City" (289).

Lisca writes that the aforementioned Krutch review of *Eden*, and another by Mark Schorer not included in Tedlock and Wicker, reflect "a certain ambivalence which is an accurate index to the peculiar effect of Steinbeck's novel, one of both greatness and failure"(264). Lisca picks up on a term Steinbeck used defensively in holding that the novel only sounded "sloppy" — but really wasn't. Indeed it is, avers Lisca (265).

One might also rebut Lisca by suggesting that, in searching for a purloined letter that would explain Steinbeck's method in *Eden*, he missed what was in full sight all along. But who can fault his early noting that "the prose of *East of Eden* alternates between . . . pseudo-poetry and an abandoned, unstudied carelessness incapable of organizing the sprawling materials, and, because the narrator himself is so ambiguously defined, incapable of emphasizing them" (272–73)?

Lisca goes on to connect his disappointment with changes in Steinbeck's approach:

> As the failure of prose style is allied to the failure of structure, so both are allied to the new emphasis on character. In *East of Eden*, for the first time since *Cup of Gold*, Steinbeck is concerned with his characters primarily as individuals who exist and have importance apart from the materials of his novel, for it is through them rather than through structure and language that he tries to establish his theme. . . . Steinbeck fails because his characters are neither credible as individuals nor effective as types but are an incongruous mixture of both. (273)

Yes? And? But it is easy with the hindsight of forty years to venture cavils on issues still unresolved about a book whose "pioneer" stature is indisputable.

A writer and critic whose experience with Steinbeck seems to have been shaped by the Second World War is Warren French, once also like Peter Lisca at the University of Florida. Deputized to write only the second number of Twayne's lengthy United States Authors Series, French made his own attempt to solve the Steinbeck puzzle. An

anonymous writer of the jacket cover blurb put a finger on John Steinbeck's wavering stature in 1961 in noting that "John Steinbeck's rapid
rise to the top rank of American writers and his equally rapid plunge
from this eminence have been among the most remarkable phenomena
in American literary history." The same notes promise that French will
explain how Steinbeck lost a lot of his gift when "the author abandoned
his native California for the big city; a country boy at heart, Steinbeck
has only recently begun to understand the city well enough to write
about it as authoritatively as he did about the simple people and dramatic problems of his native region." This language is not only dated
but condescending in several directions.

In fact, French's preface begins with a speculation about why John
Steinbeck "is not so often mentioned [as] respectfully in discussions of
American fiction as Faulkner, Hemingway, and Fitzgerald; if the will of
some literary historians prevailed, he would be relegated to a footnote"
(French 7). Again, the defensive mode of the first generation of Steinbeck critics; again, the dismissive "country boy" motif. French's was to
be part of the "footnote."

French was writing under the constraints of a tighter series format
than mine, and had as much reason as Lisca to observe a strictly
chronological survey of Steinbeck's work. He was also able to cover all
but the last volume of Steinbeck's fiction, *The Winter of Our Discontent*. French is, at this stage, less sympathetic than Lisca to the Steinbeck of the 1940s and 1950s; but it is not hard to find in this relative
dismissiveness a strategy for retaining high respect for what French considers to have been the best of Steinbeck. French, who did service during the War, seems to long for the good old days before that conflict,
much like Tennessee Williams's Tom Wingfield. That Steinbeck also
did foxhole time as a correspondent was no excuse in French's eyes for
apparently having repudiated the lower classes — as if Steinbeck had
ever done so.

French's preface is very much a piece of its time, even when he de-
fends a Steinbeck "condemned for not being Kafka or Becket" (*sic*, 7).
On the other hand, this editor — or French — was prescient in guess-
ing at Steinbeck's post-modernist mode without yet being able to identify it.

Yet French is undeniably rough on the middle-period Steinbeck,
even if only in the interests of shoring up the reputation of the "literary
landmarks" he produced in the 1930s. He is also generous in praising
the last work for which he seems to have had patience, *Cannery Row*.

He describes in it precisely the qualities he would later miss in Steinbeck's fiction:

> The enemy Steinbeck attacks — the destructive force that preys on the world — is, as usual in his novels, respectability: the desire to attain an unnatural security for one's self by ruthlessly disregarding the feelings of others. (120)

And so when this craving for respectability, this desire to be secure in an insecure world, becomes a primal motive in the characters of Steinbeck's later fiction, Steinbeck seems, in French's eyes, to have betrayed his authorial trust.

French somehow cottoned to the "combined method" by which Steinbeck created *Cannery Row,* and thereby refused to dismiss it as simply "a classic of American humor" (121). It is in this sense a shame that French decided to do a chapter-by-chapter structural analysis of a book that was and is, by self-definition, an accounting of chaos. French is sharpest when he is not trying to be ingenious and treating his chosen text as some sort of cabala or numbers game. Without naming him, he refutes for all time Edmund Wilson's stupid categorization of Steinbeck as a writer who equated humans and animals:

> . . . but exactly what he is attempting to do in the last two chapters of *Cannery Row* is to distinguish men from the other animals — or at least to indicate that men have capabilities available to no other animals, if they will but avail themselves of them. (134)

Thus Warren French seems to have been on the verge of a major discovery about the later Steinbeck and about where the author was going. It seems to have been a standard rubric of Steinbeck criticism in the 1950s and 1960s to have pled on the writer's behalf while at the same time nailing theses to the cathedral door: Here I stand; after this there is no reading the man.

It is interesting that the slightly earlier Lisca accepted the 1940s Steinbeck works, whereas French writing slightly later would reject them. But one must remember that in this time frame, no one was talking about John Steinbeck except at some sort of article-length parameter; and that Lisca and French were in fact pioneers and deserve to be recognized as such.

In 1962, the first guide to John Steinbeck's work by a British critic was published, F. W. Watt's *John Steinbeck*. Like Warren French's volume, it bore as its title the name of its subject, though Watt had apparently not been able to make use of French's book before issuing his own. Watt's study is an example of the paperback book's golden age; its

117 pages easily fit into the back pocket of a graduate student's jeans. What is most refreshing about Watt's approach is that, aware as he is of nearly all prior Steinbeck criticism, he nonetheless brings an outsider's perspective to bear, one not shaped or warped by the regional biases of North America. Thus for Watt, John Steinbeck's departure from the West Coast in the early 1940s was less an abandonment, a fatal distraction, than simply "the era of travel" (Watt 9).

Watt also seems to have been the first foreign critic to have read all the work that Steinbeck would publish in his lifetime, that is, all of the fiction. Eager as he is to praise fairness in previous critics, Watt is also sturdily fair in his own judgments — balanced but independent, and at his best when venturing from plot summary, a trait that no doubt is owing to the desire to familiarize British readers with a very different sort of writer than they were used to.

And Watt is remarkably open-minded about such later writings as *Sweet Thursday* and *The Short Reign of Pippin IV,* giving them their due in brief coverage while respectfully reading them in the light of Steinbeck's apparent intentions instead of dismissing them out of hand. But later, sensing the ambitiousness of Steinbeck's final novel, *The Winter of Our Discontent,* he responds with fitting seriousness to a book that had as yet received little critical attention, noting that

> . . . private and public morality, Good Friday and the Fourth of July, Ethan's and modern America's decline and corruption, are to be related within Ethan's capacious psyche. But the final effect is rather of double-exposure, raising the questions: What sort of person is Ethan really? How wise and how foolish? How seriously are we to take him? Steinbeck has never used the first-person narrator before, and the cause of his difficulties seems to be that he found he could identify himself with the "I" in Ethan's wisdom, but not in his folly; hence Ethan's temptation and fall from innocence are factitious and unconvincing. (103)

This is fair and perceptive, if debatable; for instance, it can surely be argued that Steinbeck's strategy forces Ethan's existential dilemma upon the reader's own consciousness, or conscience.

But Watt is writing of *Winter* early on and under severe space constraints which I will discuss later. And we remember that his subject is a living author — hence Watt's use of the present tense. As he concludes,

> Steinbeck called *Cannery Row* a "mixed-up book" but *The Winter of Our Discontent* is much more so. It leaves one, nevertheless, with a sense of new, troubled, unchannelled power beneath its smooth surfaces which goes some way to justify Steinbeck's refusal to build on

old foundations or to be bound by his "long valley," and which points to a continuing struggle for understanding and expression. For this energetic, determined, and prolific author, now at three-score years, shows no signs yet of having had his say. (103)

Alas, not so; but Watt's positive attitude prophesies a new generation of Steinbeck readership.

Watt also leaves "to autobiography or a future biographer" questions such as the ultimate effect on Steinbeck's work of "the several marriages" (9). Watt could not have been sure that he had in fact in his defense of the writer, as when he argues that the "literary slummers" who first misread *Tortilla Flat* "could enjoy the off-beat, colorful, uninhibited, irresponsible behavior of the paisanos while at the same time criticizing, explicitly or implicitly, the aspects of respectable society which make the holiday life of those beyond its bounds so attractive" (39). Though Watt is eager to call this device of Steinbeck's a bit of a "formula," the term is interesting in view of Watt's date of publication: that same graduate student might well have been carrying Grove Press's Henry Miller volumes in his or her other jeans pocket. On the other hand, Watt is ahead of himself and his times when he opines that in *Tortilla Flat,* Steinbeck "draws attention away from those sordid aspects upon which realism would have to dwell more fully" (41).

Thus though Watt seems to expect Steinbeck to have carried the Rickettsian motto until death, he seems open to the possibility that Steinbeck was ready to move off in his own directions. But Watt seems also to have been seriously influenced by Peter Lisca; the works of the 1940s are given due respect, as they are not given in French's first study. *Burning Bright* gets little more than a page since as Watt sees it, "*Burning Bright* plainly illustrates the loss of certainty and sustenance experienced at so great a distance from the people and soil of Steinbeck's 'long valley'" (93). There it is again; when in doubt about how to blame John Steinbeck for a new sin, target the moving van.

One can only wonder what sort of rush to print might have overtaken F. W. Watt to the extent that he covered such a clearly ambitious novel — on the scale of *The Grapes of Wrath* — as *East of Eden* in a mere half dozen pages. But in any case the three American critics of John Steinbeck who contributed volumes during the 1960s surpassed his work in terms of coverage if not in terms of objectivity, and they constitute the first generation of serious Steinbeck commentary: Peter Lisca, Warren French and (to come) Joseph Fontenrose.

Warren French's *A Companion to "The Grapes of Wrath"* rode on the strength of his own thorough study of Steinbeck's fiction. French's assemblage of essays (1963) may be only the second of its kind, but it has also by now been surpassed by subsequent collections of previously published articles. In fact, French's anthology perhaps instantly dated itself by relying overmuch on initial receptions of a novel that, even in 1963, some readers expected to be in the end Steinbeck's only "book."

French's volume reflects the tenor of the times in which it was assembled. Compiled one year after Steinbeck was awarded the Nobel Prize for Literature, it seeks to justify that award largely in terms of the accuracy of Steinbeck's reportage. Over thirty years later, hardly any reader cares whether Steinbeck got the birds and the snakes and the flowers of Oklahoma wrong or right, because his construct, *The Grapes of Wrath,* had long since replaced "reality" in the minds of its readers. As the present millennium winds down, French's compilation seems meant to reassure the young that, roughly, Yes, Virginia, there was a Dust Bowl and a subsequent migration.

Warren French's *Companion,* for all of the relatively conservative choices the editor makes for inclusion, does reflect the nature of what was available at the time; and it also places *Grapes* in temporal and geographic contexts, that is, not simply a literary one. Moreover, it became the model for Peter Lisca's critical editions of the novel to follow, as well as for other essay collections that focus on this single work.

This survey, having reached 1963, will end its first chapter by considering Joseph Fontenrose's *John Steinbeck: An Introduction and Interpretation,* written for John Mahoney's American Authors and Critics series for Holt, Rinehart and Winston. It is fitting that the last title issued before a five-year hiatus in book-length Steinbeck studies be Fontenrose's, for not only was it the last of the three or four major studies that prompted the attentions of a second and more specialized wave of Steinbeck readers, but it marks the end of an era in yet another way: in its able response to the constraints of a series format, it reminds us that not since Harry Thornton Moore, almost a quarter of a century earlier, had a scholar and critic been free to conduct a thoroughly independent study of Steinbeck without the sometimes dubious benefits of contractual demands.

Fontenrose is particularly keen on the subject of myth and science as part of Steinbeck's earliest influences, and thus he is less open to the moralistic tendencies, as he sees them, of the later works. Indeed, it's all he can do to restrain himself from judging them negatively. Without seeming to understand that any sort of stylistic changes might also have been going on in Steinbeck's fiction, Fontenrose takes his cue from Peter Lisca (Warren French's study seems to have been published too late for inclusion in Fontenrose's lucubrations): "In Steinbeck's novels biology takes the place of history, mysticism takes the place of humanism" (Fontenrose 140).

But Fontenrose hurriedly avers that he is referring to the earlier works he most respects:

> As if aware of something unsatisfactory in his point of view, Steinbeck turned from biology to a vague moralism, which proved even more unsatisfactory, since it was not derived from a penetrating study of men interacting in society. He saw the world more whole when he saw it biologically. (141)

Thus even the early titles are guilty of "philosophic shortcomings," but still "the earlier novels are great novels" (141). Fontenrose is unique among earlier Steinbeck critics in insisting on his own private definition of "philosophy," which embraces myth, science, and even secular religion but rejects any form of prescriptive moralism. Fontenrose must have found in the early Steinbeck a kindred spirit willing to adhere to a toughminded materialism akin to Robinson Jeffers's or to some of Hawthorne's more perverse protagonists, but certainly averse to anything resembling metaphysics. As he concludes of Steinbeck,

> In several ways he has asserted that all life is holy, every creature valuable. Herein lies his sentimentality, but also his strength. His great novels, like *The Grapes of Wrath,* will endure for their narrative power and strength of vision. (141)

This statement raises the issue of whether for some critics such as Joseph Fontenrose there might have lurked, in his garden of myth, a form of sentimentalism he and prior critics never suspected, their own sentimentalism and not John Steinbeck's.

Fontenrose is happiest when Steinbeck reverts to his early myth- and philosophy-based style, what Steinbeck and Ricketts were calling "nonteleological" thinking, essentially a rejection of any metaphysical interference with things as they are. Thus he is pleased that, despite his claims to be telling a black-and-white, good-and-bad type of retold tale in *The Pearl,* Steinbeck cannot stop the earlier mode of thinking from asserting itself:

> As one might expect in a tale that grew out of *Sea of Cortez,* Steinbeck's interest in biology is more evident than in his other novels of the forties. Here is the town that "is a thing like a colonial animal," which "has a whole emotion," and through which news travels swiftly by mysterious channels. The news of Kino's pearl "stirred up something infinitely black and evil in the town; the black distillate was like

the scorpion . . . The poison sacs of the town began to manufacture venom, and the town swelled and puffed with the pressure of it." The town as organism is plainly Leviathan, who will root out any troublesome member. And in the town as ecological unit each kind of inhabitant — pearl fishers, pearl buyers, Spanish aristocrats, beggars, ants, dogs — has its niche, its particular means of preserving itself. And each individual must stay within the niche of his kind and not encroach on another's. (114)

Fontenrose embraces a hard gospel here willingly, and yet he also provides an answer to readers who have found Steinbeck's treatment of Kino cruel: Individuals cannot advance, only species can.

But Fontenrose's study stands defined by such initial statements as the one in his chapter 8, "The Moralities," where he makes evident his animus towards the Steinbeck who had somehow "changed" on him:

Now the great days are done. Since *The Grapes of Wrath* and *Sea of Cortez* Steinbeck has written nine novels and four other books. Each has received varied responses from critics and readers; each has had its defenders; but in general the nay-sayers have been more numerous. (98)

Which, from our perspective, means precisely what? If Joseph Fontenrose was not exactly caving in to majority rule in 1963, what indeed was he about? It does not seem to have entered his mind that even in 1963, literature was not a democratic state. What if Steinbeck were a prophet?

Thus we come to the end of a quarter-century of "pioneer" critics who blazed the trails for all who came after. From the early 1960s onward, it became possible to specialize in and "profess" Steinbeck studies. The next chapter will demonstrate as much in the process of dealing with twice as many writers, some the peers, and some not, of their predecessors. As a Willa Cather critic would note, a pioneer generation may invest itself in the land, and a subsequent one treat it as real estate. But Steinbeck studies have always required resilience, whether from those who settled Okie country at the turn of the century or those who trekked westward a third of a century later. So too with Steinbeck's critics; a second generation would find bones and brush in their path, but also plenty of wheel-ruts to lead them on.

Works Consulted

Fontenrose, Joseph. *John Steinbeck: An Introduction and Interpretation*. New York: Holt, Rinehart and Winston, 1963.

French, Warren. *John Steinbeck*. New York: Twayne, 1961.

——, ed. *A Companion to "The Grapes of Wrath."* New York: Viking, 1963.

Gannett, Lewis. *John Steinbeck: Personal and Bibliographical Notes*. New York: Viking, 1939.

——, ed. *The Portable Steinbeck*. New York: Viking, 1946.

Lisca, Peter. *The Wide World of John Steinbeck*. New Brunswick, NJ: Rutgers UP, 1958.

Moore, Harry Thornton. *The Novels of John Steinbeck: A First Study*. Chicago: Normandie House, 1939.

Tedlock, E. W., Jr., and C. V. Wicker, eds. *Steinbeck and His Critics*. Albuquerque: U New Mexico P, 1957.

Watt, F. W. *John Steinbeck*. New York: Grove, 1962.

2: Caretakers

FROM THE LATE 1960s TO THE LATE 1970s there was obviously a new movement in Steinbeck studies. Aside from the appearance and widespread influence of the *Steinbeck Quarterly* at the end of the first decade, a phenomenon to be covered separately in chapter three, it is clear that after the death of the writer a new generation of critics felt free to go off in new directions.

Conversely, it just might also have been time for new writers, critics, and editors, tired of smoothing over the old sand traps, to make and leave their own distinctive prints and spoors. Yet there remained a steady market for the sorting-out of previously published pieces, as perhaps will always be the case. In December of 1968 John Steinbeck died at sixty-six after a series of cardiovascular traumas, and suddenly one generation's fair game became whatever another might make of him.

This is not to suggest that much of the work done in this period did not reflect heartfelt appreciation for Steinbeck's writing or exhibit occasional original brilliance.

In 1967, Robert L. Gale published yet another study guide, *Barron's Simplified Approach to Steinbeck: "Grapes of Wrath."* The title gives the game away. To simplify a readily understandable book for some unknowable but presumably immature audience that probably never existed is also likely a cry of desperation. With the easy perspective that three decades allow, Gale's title was most probably forced upon him.

One must wonder whom Gale perceived to be his audience thirty years ago; he almost seems to be defending himself against livid parents when he writes, most colorfully, that

> Steinbeck is such a roughneck that most readers simply cannot believe that he is the master of a dozen literary styles, running all the way from crudities . . . to incantatory prose having Biblical sonorousness. The crudity has to be there, because Steinbeck is writing realistically about unwashed primitives who have been brutalized by fierce nature and starvation wages. (Gale 74)

We should leave Gale to his time and not tax him for seeing fit to defend Steinbeck for being a "roughneck" and for writing about "unwashed primitives," most of whom Gale's readership would have become by the time his manual saw print.

In 1968, that same year of Steinbeck's death and, as he would have been quick to remind you, an epically chaotic one, Agnes McNeill Donohue published *A Casebook on "The Grapes of Wrath,"* with some of the usual suspects, but Donohue lets the reader hear from some refreshingly new voices as well. As with French's *Companion,* Donohue tries to set *Grapes* into a temporal and spatial context as well as a literary one, but her range of chosen reprints is much larger, and she is also clearly gearing her collection towards student readers, with appended questions for classroom (or homework assignment) use. The questions are premised on the optimistic assumption that students will have read not only *Grapes* but the specific included critics; and one must shake one's head at the assumptions the bogeymen of the critics she rightly catches in the act of simply being their often unimaginative selves.

But the critics she includes are by no means simply vintage voices. Many date from an era relatively close to Donohue's own date of publication, and if the editor displays any sort of predilection that some readers would hold against her sortie, it might lie with her preference for religious analyses of Steinbeck's writings that he himself, using such motifs as a rule ironically, might have disparaged. Yet such an essay as Edwin M. Moseley's of 1962 (the original print date), "Christ as the Brother of Man," draws deeply on a Woody Guthrie lyric of the forties describing a returned Christ being put to death again:

> This Christ figure of the 'thirties is in the last analysis a kind of melodramatic, if moving, hero who represents the potential goodness in man. There is little emphasis on his playing the part of scapegoat for the follies of the people who deny him his savior function . . . Casy's death may not have occurred if the workers, even though hungry, had completely supported him in the strike that he preached, but Steinbeck's attention is considerably less to the failures of the people than to the increased strength which they achieve through Casy's martyrdom. (Donohue 216–17)

Moseley's analysis seems, after this long, naïve but fair — and refreshingly on point at this present time when professional associations are much more interested in gender issues and theory than they are in the study of literature itself.

But at least a new generation of Steinbeck readers and critics was beginning to speak out, and independently. A major star that appeared in 1969 was Lester Jay Marks, a critic whose *Thematic Design in the Novels of John Steinbeck* was really the first attempt to set Steinbeck's philosophical notions against the structures of the novelist's works, without prejudice, to see whether they worked for their intended purposes.

Marks is one of the first critics who actually takes Steinbeck's writing as a given that should be examined on its own terms without applying to it any preconditional critical theory. He discovers "three thematic patterns that recur consistently, though with unequal emphasis, throughout Steinbeck's novels":

> The first of these patterns indicates that man is a religious creature and that each man creates a godhead to satisfy his personal religious need. The second pattern suggests that mankind may also be viewed biologically, as a "group animal" composed of individuals ("cells") but having a will and intelligence of its own, distinct from any one of its parts. However, outside the group is another kind of individual, analogous to the biologist himself, who, in the role of Steinbeck's constant hero, observes and comments upon the "animal." The final pattern in the thematic scheme illustrates the "non-teleological" concept that man lives without knowledge of the cause of his existence; nevertheless, the very mystery of life spurs his search for human values. (Marks 11)

Marks's approach brought in much-needed fresh air to Steinbeck studies; no more would theories have to be provided merely out of the writings of Steinbeck himself or tested in terms of their "suitability" for whatever the times seemed to dictate. And he was fortunate enough to have been able to make a contribution decades before an application to graduate school required profession of a theoretical or critical school, much like the bizarre "loyalty oaths" that some students were required to take in the early 1960s.

Marks is thus one of the first critics of Steinbeck to identify the fairly constant presence of a "Ricketts-figure" in the novelist's work. Though Marks was not ready to see such a figure as particularly distanced from the novelist's own thinking, he did readily identify such a character's dispassion:

> . . . Always in Steinbeck's novels . . . is another figure who looms outside and above the group. Viewing the group with detached compassion is always Steinbeck's prototypical biologist-philosopher. As biologist he observes the "animal" with scientific objectivity, hoping to discover in its behavior an order and a meaning within an ecological framework. As philosopher, still concerned with order and meaning, but knowing that objective reality is only part of the truth, he frees himself of conventional scientific restrictions and allows himself the luxury of subjectivity; he views the group as men who, like him-

self, are spiritual beings seeking their place within a mysteriously or-
dered cosmos. But this hero is a character in his own right, and as a
character he is loved, respected, feared, and misunderstood by the
others. He is loved because he gives solace to the weak; he is respected because he lends himself to the causes of the group and helps
to keep it alive; he is feared and misunderstood because he remains
the outsider who never seems to wholly believe in the mundane
causes of the group, and because his attitudes and methods transcend
the group's understanding. (18)

Likely no one has put this consistent presence better.

A curious next volume, or simply "essay" as its publisher calls it, is
1970's *John Steinbeck* by John Pratt, part of a "Contemporary Writers
in Christian Perspective" series from the Michigan-based William B.
Eerdmans firm. At forty-eight pages (including bibliography), the
"essay" is admittedly brief; but it is also lively enough (especially in its
wordplay between "teleological" and "theological") to make the disin-
terested reader wish it could have gone on longer and explored its subject more fully, for until recently, conventional religion as a viable (if
undogmatic) aspect of Steinbeck's writing has been largely dismissed if
not simply ignored.

Pratt's commentary is by no means bound by strictures of creed; indeed, instead of being remotely sectarian, he rather mildly notes that
Steinbeck's references to religion show that the writer

> . . . views formal religion, particularly Christianity, in two ways. First,
> a religion is one of man's basic needs and can "work" for many. But
> like any social institution that demands adherence to tradition and
> form, religion can become ironically and tragically one of the most
> unsatisfactory, perhaps even destructive means of apprehending the
> reality of existence. (Pratt 18)

This is a gentle and apt retrofitting of the insights of an ecumenical era
to the writings of someone whose childhood religious experiences were
apparently far more narrowly partisan and even fierce.

In the same year (1970), Richard O'Connor published a volume
intended for young readers, *John Steinbeck*. It must be said at the outset
that O'Connor's book has nothing of the condescending about it; and
like its contemporary from Pratt, it makes the reader wish for more,
even if its type-face and wide margins do seem to allow overmuch for
post-cafeteria thumbprints. Given his readership, O'Connor is not interested in controversy, and he is primarily concerned with getting the
facts out for a limited audience.

And yet O'Connor never talks down to his audience, and his choice of language indicates a respect for younger readers. Furthermore, as regards theme, O'Connor does not hold back out of a false sense of prudence; consider his discussion of Lennie and George and their relationship in *Of Mice and Men:*

> The tenderness of the relationship between the two men was never equaled, in Steinbeck's writings, by the relationship of his men and women. His inability to portray effectively the love of a man for a woman, or his unwillingness, was a trait he shared with other great American writers. He did create several effective women characters, but Steinbeck's essentially was a man's world. And like many masculine types, he was baffled by the intricacies of female behavior. (O'Connor 54)

Although this is accurate, it is by no means O'Connor's original discovery, but it is surprising to see these comments directed towards younger readers.

John Steinbeck's work in the film industry, as well as the film adaptations (including those for television) of his works, is a large enough topic to have commanded the attention of a number of writers who are not normally critics of fiction (with some exceptions). In some instances, filmings of Steinbeck works have been objective and accurate and by no means vacantly reverential; to that extent, they make for valuable supplemental materials for teachers of Steinbeck's works, though they are by no means substitutes for his texts.

Thus it is in that context that we consider, however briefly, a survey by an English non-academic author named Michael Burrows and published in 1971: *John Steinbeck and His Films.* Burrows has neither time nor space for much depth, and his volume could be matched for overall quality of presentation and sophistication of format by many a home publisher today. Yet his choice of stills is rich enough and his commitment genuine enough to make him another sort of "pioneer" for present purposes, even though his little aficionado's study might be almost impossible to locate anymore.

In fact, Burrows relies almost wholly on canned quotes from reviews and the like; his little manual is the sort of commentary a Steinbeck/film buff like Robert Morsberger, to be met with shortly, could probably toss off in his sleep.

In the same year (1971), Viking Press decided to issue a "revised and enlarged edition" of *The Portable Steinbeck,* edited by Pascal Covici, Jr., the son of Steinbeck's patient and encouraging longtime editor. The younger Covici taught for many years at Southern Methodist University, and thus he brings academic credentials to bear in making his choices that are well grounded in an understanding of Steinbeck's philosophy. Yet he modestly defers to his father's own statements about what makes literature exciting: that at its best, it is an "expression of the joy of living"; that it "stimulated" the "imagination" while stirring new "emotions and thoughts" within him that he was glad to find there (Covici xi). Next he defers again, this time to the writer himself, who had addressed the senior Covici in his *East of Eden* journals as being in awe of a new "awareness" that occasionally happens to the reader and leaves that person without words to explain why (xii).

Thus Covici's initial homages are carried out in his choices of selections for inclusion. The introduction is brief and concise. Only *Of Mice and Men* and *The Red Pony* remain in complete form. War-related material has been replaced by choices from Steinbeck's final works of significance, but that leaves an interesting hiatus between the early writings and most of the later selections, which deal heavily in social observation. Not surprisingly, then, the final entry is the Nobel Prize acceptance speech. But overall, this is a judicious selection representing its times. The critical reader might be excused for wondering whether there will be a third (or, in effect, fourth) version one day, and what it will be given to contain.

Covici's assertions are finally mild, speculative ones of the if-only-Mozart-had-lived-to-be-sixty sort, and not strikingly creative, however valid:

> One may wonder what John Steinbeck's preoccupations might have become had he lived longer and, therefore, written more. The group and the "one big soul" of his earlier writings make one form of an American transcendentalism that Emerson and Whitman would recognize, especially in its monistic morality that stays clear of such dualistic absolutes as "sin" and "virtue," seeing instead what Preacher Casy calls the "stuff folks do." In his later work, beginning with *Burning Bright* (1950), he concentrated his focus upon the smaller group of the family and came to emphasize a responsibility less ecological than moral. Throughout his career, echoes of Malory's *Morte d'Arthur* are never far from his consciousness, most explicitly in the modernized version of the tales on which he worked through the late 1950s. Perhaps this particular interest would have carried him to some way of combining the sense of passionate commitment of *The Grapes of Wrath* with the passionate commitment to freedom of *East of Eden* and to responsibility in *The Winter of Our Discontent*. But any such speculation has value only in so far as it adds to a savoring of what John Steinbeck did in fact achieve. In literature, emotional truth,

moral value, and social relevance all come down to life upon the page, to the author's capacity to create, and thus to vivify, the experience of being human. Because John Steinbeck had this capacity, his work should long give to his readers the delight in which all lasting art has its beginning and its end. (xxix)

Covici here is clearly a man doing an assigned job, breaking no new ground, and speaking in the temporal context of a recent Nobel Prize reception. The tentative tone is thus present to be understood and passed over.

It may say something about the tenor of these same times that when James Gray's *John Steinbeck* appeared in the same year (1971), it was as another series title, this time in fact a series pamphlet of little over forty pages of text. The series involved, University of Minnesota Pamphlets on American Writers, mostly from the present century, was designed especially for student use; and yet it says something about the Minnesota's Press's enthusiasm for John Steinbeck that Gray's title appears as "No. 94" in the sequence; in other words, the Steinbeck assignment must have been made twice as far into the series as the one of John P. Marquand and almost forty titles after James Gould Cozzens had been attended to.

Clearly Steinbeck's standing had fallen, or was perceived as having fallen, over the past couple of decades, leaving Gray free to be dismissive of the writer. In fairness to him, it must be said that he did not do so. Gray is by no means a Steinbeck specialist, but there are few academic institutions where true Steinbeck specialists can ply their trade. Because he has little space for detailed book-by-book coverage, Gray relies on elucidating overall themes that come and go throughout Steinbeck's work. This makes him something of a generalizer, a critic concentrating on authorial philosophy, a trait common to many of Steinbeck's commentators. It also makes him a bit of a casual name-dropper, prone as he is to seek for influences and comparisons.

Thus as he approaches his conclusion, Gray calls the writer "a kind of working Freudian," but not a doctrinaire one. Gray goes on to credit Steinbeck for exploring "the suggestions" of Freud and Frazer, and for covering a far broader field than did his fellow writers; he continues:

His was an ambitious and inclusive effort to relate contemporary evidence about "the human condition" to that of the great witnesses of the past. His work suggests again and again that the story of humankind is a steadily continuing one, full of passions that seem as familiar in a setting of two thousand years ago as they do in our own time. It is the sense of the past made present that gives Steinbeck's best books their universality of tone. Old perils the like of which still surround us, old aspirations renewed . . . are the elements that contribute the essence of drama to his stories and give him distinction. (Gray 45)

It is Gray's well-stated tribute to Steinbeck's *historical* universality that distinguishes his understanding of the writer's mythic sense in the end:

> Steinbeck, the analyst and critic of society, had in his time to refute many charges of bias against democracy and "the American way of life." Consideration of his work on this level of its interest may well begin with a listing of the kinds of influence he did not aspire to exert. He was never a radical thinker, pamphleteer, agitator, Communist, or fellow traveler. (31)

Now there appeared a particularly distinguished and ultimately influential study, one also of note for apparent freedom from publisher-imposed inhibition. (Interestingly, it was also issued by Minnesota.) A young professor at Oregon State University named Richard Astro, working on a university grant and another from the NEH (National Endowment for the Humanities) and with the cooperation of many Steinbeck intimates, brought out *John Steinbeck and Edward F. Ricketts: The Shaping of a Novelist*. Those intimates, including a former wife (Gwyndolyn Conger) and sundry kinds of pals, drinking or scientific or both, have of course been diminishing in number in the nearly three decades since Astro did his research, making his interviews and recollections of them all the more precious.

The significance of Ricketts to Steinbeck's early thinking and, therefore, his influence on the early writing had long been understood in general terms, such as in the earlier studies by Peter Lisca and Joseph Fontenrose; but the nature of the proportionate interchanges of ideas and values between Ricketts and Steinbeck could only have been guessed at. For example, it was clear enough that there was a "Ricketts" figure in many of Steinbeck's fictions; indeed, it might be argued that there is always one of them present. But not until recent years has it been noted how often Steinbeck makes a Hitchcockian personal appearance in his own stories, which certainly complicates any attempt to make either man seem the model for a protagonist seen in a positive light. The Ricketts types, for example, are often self-sidelined philosophizers who disappear at the point of action; the "Steinbecks" can be weak and flawed.

Astro states at the beginning:

> Earlier studies of Steinbeck's philosophy of life have been shortsighted and incomplete. Despite some apparent contradictions, Stein-

beck's world-view contains a meaningful statement about the human condition which is consistent with his major talent for depicting nature and man. And until Steinbeck's view of man and the world is stated clearly and honestly, there is no way of assessing properly the full measure of his contribution to American letters. (Astro 4)

Astro reminds the reader how strenuously Steinbeck objected to being given sole credit for writing *Sea of Cortez,* with only scientific contributions by Edward F. Ricketts being noted in the book's huge "appendix." The book recounts, and results from, the exploratory journey to the Gulf of California the two men took in the *Western Flyer* in 1940. (The account was published in 1941). Made as the Second World War was already underway in Europe, the trip was more than ostensibly made for serious marine-biological research purposes; yet it also not only proved to be, by all witness accounts, something of a movable feast, but the book's "log" was later published by itself in 1951, along with Steinbeck's memoir about his friend, "About Ed Ricketts," after he was killed in a grade-crossing accident in Monterey in 1948. Thus it became doubly easy to presume (and wish) that the significant parts of both texts were John Steinbeck's (14).

Astro would have no part of a deception that, to his credit, Steinbeck himself also refused. Instead of supporting such a comfortable delusion, Astro places in context the complementarity of thought between Steinbeck and Ricketts up until this time, but for not very long afterwards. It is clear enough that Steinbeck was the better writer, but the question of who is the dominant thinker can be resolved only by means of individual investigation of the available evidence Astro provides for the first time:

> . . . the intellectual side of the Steinbeck-Ricketts relationship is a highly complex matter, and it is necessary to identify those issues on which the two men disagreed as well as those occasions on which Steinbeck simply fictionalized the philosophical premises of his best friend. (27)

And this Astro proceeds to do, moving in a novel way through the Steinbeck canon that was, by this time, more or less complete.

For instance, even though writers such as this one might argue that Steinbeck weaned himself from the Rickettsian domination throughout the 1940s and especially after Ricketts's death, there is no gainsaying the validity of Astro's comment on the final works: "It was largely through Ricketts' eyes that Steinbeck learned how to see natural beauty and how to intuit from nature fundamental truths about the relational unity of all life" (218).

In the end, Astro makes a compelling case for the argument that Ricketts's influence was a central factor in the novelist's becoming his own man:

> By analyzing the range and depth of Ricketts' impact on Steinbeck's fiction, one may see Steinbeck's accomplishments as a writer with fresh perspective. The novelist's philosophy of life is not tenth-rate, and his social and political material is not worn and obsolete. In his best works, Steinbeck fused science and philosophy, art and ethics, by combining the broad-visioned and compelling metaphysic of Edward F. Ricketts with a personal gospel of social action. In his own time and with his own voice, John Steinbeck defined and gave meaning to the uniquely complicated nature of human experience. (230)

One cannot evade this continuing emphasis on Steinbeck's philosophy, certainly an almost unique sidebar in the history of literary/biographical studies, perhaps an unprecedentedly obsessive one among Steinbeck critics; yet Richard Astro's study is necessary reading for those hoping to get a genuine grasp of what is going on underneath the surface of Steinbeck's deceptively "simple" fiction.

In 1972, there appeared Peter Lisca's *John Steinbeck: "The Grapes of Wrath": Text and Criticism*. Lisca's volume is a template for other volumes on other writers to follow. It contains Viking's then-current in-print text of the novel, a map of the Joads' exodus, four contextual articles on the work's initial social significance, and eleven newer pieces with a more literary focus. Naturally, at this early stage of scholarship Lisca's first edition could not have included the corrected text he was able to employ on his second essay (see below), just as there is limited space for the inclusion of reprinted articles; and to that end, Lisca relies in the main on important pieces that appeared too late for his dissertation, and his first book. But there are also the newer entries, and of course the requisite questions for essay and classroom discussion purposes — and also an impressively full bibliography. Designed for bright undergraduates or Master's students, Lisca's anthology remained an authority for at least a generation.

To complete the survey of 1972's contributions to Steinbeck studies, we need consider Robert Murray Davis's *Steinbeck: A Collection of Critical Essays,* compiled for Prentice-Hall's extensive Twentieth Century Views series, one well known as a friend to desperate writers of term papers. Davis's inclusions indicate a predisposition towards the earlier works, not surprising for his time. But what is particularly interesting in his introduction is how Davis, for whatever personal reasons, seems to admire Steinbeck's nuts-and-bolts interest in the small manual tasks on the basis of which the planet runs (Davis 11).

Nonetheless, although Davis has some personal favorites among Steinbeck's fictions that many would disagree with (*To a God Unknown* and *The Wayward Bus,* for example), he feels constrained by his times to be harsh, grudging, and hedging of his bets overall:

> . . . All of Steinbeck's critics agree that much of his work cannot endure, is indeed stillborn. Except for *The Sea of Cortez,* his nonfiction is mediocre to dreadful; almost everything written after 1947 is seriously flawed, primarily in the strained quality of the prose. However, many of his books still live, in the sense that they are read, discussed, and reprinted, and at least some of them may last beyond this admittedly marginal existence. (15)

Note that for Davis, 1947 is a magical cutoff date in Steinbeck's output. He does not explain why, nor does he (any more than most critics of the period) really deal with Steinbeck's annoying habit of producing works that continue to be "read, discussed, and reprinted," as if out of spite.

Yet to be evenhanded to Davis even insofar as he is being evenhanded, his defense of *To a God Unknown* and *The Wayward Bus* is so spirited and spunky as to defy the conventional critical thinking of the era:

> . . . *To a God Unknown* and *The Wayward Bus* are generally scorned. Both have flaws, but the first evokes the natural world and the man's kinship to it with a freshness that Steinbeck was seldom to surpass, and it conveys with a quirky, engaging, and slightly overblown style Steinbeck's most characteristic themes. The second evokes, with fascinated loathing, the grimy, sugary, and second-hand quality of postwar, pre-Holiday Inn America. Both deal with men who consciously enter traps — the one of ritual, the other of responsibility — and read in this way, they could be revalued. For now, they can serve as a touchstone for critics: anyone who purports to be a spokesman for Steinbeck but who summarily rejects both novels is not to be trusted because he cannot see the qualities that may enable Steinbeck's work to endure. (15)

This "in-your-face" assertion is from a critic who on the same page wonders whether *Grapes'* reputation might well decline as that of *In Dubious Battle* advances.

The year 1973 brought forth only two volumes of interest to the Steinbeck critic, and yet both of them have resources to offer that have not yet been tapped.

Steve Crouch published a "coffee-table" volume of photos entitled *Steinbeck Country,* with appropriate short citations from Steinbeck's writing. With the luxury of a quarter of a century's retrospect, we can admire the photos even as we are taken again with the casual splendor of the countryside that Steinbeck made famous. Even today, visitors will aver that the feminine curves of Steinbeck country, changing from spring to fall from a verdant hue to a desiccated tan, are a constituent quality in Steinbeck's writing. And perhaps no one has yet tried to assess the validity of the photographer's responses to the literature — and the landscape.

One is tempted to contrast Crouch's poetic prose with Steinbeck's own, as when he describes a favorite Steinbeck subject, the differences in tonality between the two mountain ranges that border the Salinas Valley, the Gabilans and the Santa Lucias:

> Because the Gabilans are covered most of the year with dried, yellow grasses, they have a warm, welcoming air about them, and the light on their slopes is bright and golden. By contrast, the Santa Lucias, because of their heavier vegetation and some indescribable quality of the light, are cool and blue and dark. The outlines of the lower foothills are often lost against the higher ridges beyond, so that, when seen from a distance, the peaks seem to rise straight up from the valley floor. . . . (Crouch 22)

And so on. It is interesting that Crouch's style clearly resembles Steinbeck's here and often elsewhere, probably because both men are responding honestly to a landscape. And yet the "scientific" Steinbeck insists on reading into his native valley, imputing mythic resonances and purposes to it; while Crouch is the truer scientist, seeing matters as the natural effects of geology, vegetation, and — most of all — light.

The second volume of interest to the Steinbeck critic to come out in 1973 was Warren French's *Filmguide to "The Grapes of Wrath."* French indulged in a personal interest to a degree hardly possible a few years before with this contribution to the Indiana University Press Filmguide series. Unfortunately it is not studded with stills from the movie, which was released in early 1940 and thus made remarkable quickly after the novel's publication. French does compare key scenes from both media and attempts to justify the needs of each. There seems to have been little attention paid since this slender volume's publication to the deeper implications of such comparisons, and yet film treatments of novels are an enormously popular field today, especially for students. French concludes by suggesting that the film version, even if some find the ending "sentimental," is, like the Joads themselves, still "on the road" (French, *Filmguide* 62–63), since critics still pay attention to it and still discuss its merits. A John Ford filmography is appended, along with a necessarily now-dated list of rental sources.

French is especially perceptive in noting that the film version of *The Grapes of Wrath* has not so much weakened or become dated over time as the culture that produced it has changed — at least in terms of the Okies it represented, and for there and then:

> Pearl Harbor changed every aspect of American life. Even the Okies themselves disappeared into California's burgeoning defense industries. It took the violence of war to solve the problems that men could not solve peacefully. The conditions that *The Grapes of Wrath* depicted were — to play on the title of its even more legendary competitor — "gone with the wind." Migrant labor became so scarce that California growers had to resort to the illegal importation of Mexican "wetbacks."

And French expresses the viewpoint of that mainstream "American" culture in noting that it could now avert its eyes from a problem no longer quite its own:

> *The Grapes of Wrath*, as film as well as novel, marked not the beginning of a period of social protest but its end. Zanuck and Ford were right — though surely inadvertently — in treating the story nostalgically, for *The Grapes of Wrath* looks backward not forward. It serves to remind viewers even today not of what they must do, but where they have been. (58)

And yet, it is odd to find a guide published in 1973 not reflecting more of what for almost a decade was routinely referred to as an enduring "relevance" for both novel and film.

Now the film is available in a sharp, restored VCR version for home or classroom use. Another text on Steinbeck and film will be covered later, but we should note in passing the name of a film historian whose chapters and articles appear in some of the books under consideration, though he as yet lacks a Steinbeck title of his own. Robert Morsberger has a phenomenal memory for the details of film credits and even running times, and the reader especially interested in the connection between Steinbeck and film — he was involved in a number of film projects, of course — might want to seek out Morsberger's contributions on the subject. (He edited the screenplay of *Viva Zapata!* for publication as well.)

In the following year, 1974, only one book on John Steinbeck's work appeared, but it is a major one: Howard Levant's *The Novels of John Steinbeck: A Critical Study*. Levant regards Steinbeck as a writer in search of form or, more accurately, in search of lucky marriages of form and narrative content. Because he brings his own notions of what constitutes appropriate form to bear on an idiosyncratic artist's output Levant produces the impression that he is an overbearing and even prejudiced critic delivering himself of arbitrary opinions.

Levant is undissuaded by the possibility of arousing reader rage, convinced as he is that he is doing what is best for Steinbeck's reputation, for after administering strong if bitter medicine, "We can best praise the best when we know why it is the best," he states just before his concluding paragraph:

> I do not hesitate to claim that this study will enhance, not harm, Steinbeck's reputation, for the candid reader may draw from it a sensible knowledge of Steinbeck's art and appreciate the essential unity of that art and its relevance to all of Steinbeck's longer fiction. Such knowledge is the necessary basis for perceiving the justice of evaluative judgments that rest on the accuracy, the soundness, the completeness of the evidence. Genuine distinctions of value need to claim that solid basis. I have made the claim; I trust the result is worthy. (302)

The student of Steinbeck annoyed by a critical moralist's tone here might conclude that Levant preempted the role of reviewer of his own book.

But Levant foresaw that reaction as well and had no less a person than Warren French write his book's introduction for him. French and Levant agree about the weaknesses, as they see them, of the early and late works, though they disagree about a couple of middle-period ones. French uses his temporary pulpit, however, to go after the defects in formal matters of his predecessor (but also contemporary) Peter Lisca (xii-xv), whose use of terms such as "craftsmanship" and "techniques," he finds, mean little more than an original use of language to constitute a personal style. Moreover, when Lisca refers to Steinbeck's "patterns" he seems to refer to narrational habits rather than structure, properly understood.

French argues that Joseph Fontenrose went further than Lisca without really shaking off New Critical modes of reading, so that for Fontenrose the primary critical question was "Did the artist say the right thing well?" (xvi-xvii). French states the issue with telling clarity in his conclusion when he quotes Steinbeck's Stanford instructor in the art of the story, Edith Mirrielees, as having said that the most important thing about the craft of fiction is "the thing the story is about, as apart from what merely happens in it" (xxii). And French finishes by asking "whether many times — especially in *East of Eden* and other later novels — 'the thing the story is about' may not have overwhelmed 'what happens in it,' to the detriment of the story's artistry" (xxii).

French aptly uses *The Red Pony* to illustrate both aims. He refers to Levant's approach as "constructionalist" (an interesting choice of terms, adumbrating as it does the later structuralist and deconstructionist modes of analysis; but both French and Levant have no intention of turning their backs on the importance of content, or matter); yet at a quarter-century's remove from the present the structural implications of Steinbeck's arguably postmodern, reflexive kind of narration in the later works seems not to have occurred to either critic.

Levant agrees with French, stating in his preface that "A typical defect in a Steinbeck novel is that its structure — whatever its type — is developed for its own sake, independent of the materials, to the extent that structure and materials tend to pull apart" (2–3).

Levant goes on to list typical "formal devices" that Steinbeck employs, but adds that such devices do not in themselves constitute "structure":

> At best, these devices serve to intensify the effect of a structure that is developing well, but they cannot save a structure that fails to develop properly for other reasons. Hence, they are distinctly secondary aids to order. (3)

This is undeniable as applied theory, yet also difficult to put into practice. For any reader wanting an example of formal structure made into formal stricture, Howard Levant is the critic to start with. For the rest of us, perhaps Levant has raised more issues than he can really deal with in even so detailed and complex a study as his — and maybe that is no bad thing.

It is not always clear what Levant is asserting in the conclusion to his chapter on *The Wayward Bus*, at least in its final lines; but it is certain that he differs with his predecessors as to precisely where and how to challenge Steinbeck's means and purposes. In speaking of the point in Steinbeck's career at which *Bus* was published, Levant most explicitly goes his own critical way, and in the process begins to seem like one of those resolute Steinbeck protagonists (or those of other American writers) — male, of course — determined to pursue their absolutes at any cost to psychic balance; again, speaking of *Bus* as an artistic watershed, he makes widesweeping and dire predictions:

> Steinbeck's reputation among critics commences its irrecoverably steep decline at just this point. The cause is not a sell-out, a betrayal of social concern or analysis by the most famous novelist of the Depression, for surely *The Wayward Bus* is a trenchant, accurate portrayal of the darker side of the American dream. The overwhelming sense of a failed talent in this novel is not at all thematic. The betrayal, the failure, is almost entirely artistic. The recurring charge that Steinbeck cannot handle ideas is more accurately phrased as Steinbeck's relative inability to achieve a convincing expression of ideas — a harmony of structure and materials.

And here Levant parts company with even more readers:

> . . . No doubt the comedy of sexual mannerisms is a significant theme in America. The play-novelette form is less than ideal for the expression of that theme and of most other themes. Steinbeck's inability to comprehend this crux is apparent in his dismissal of negative criticism — and in his forging on to the disaster that is *East of Eden.* (233)

But it is hard to understand, even after so long, what is wrong about premising form in matter, and writing accordingly. John Steinbeck is not known to have taken advice from critical theorists, after all. Some readers, in short, may have in the end nothing but a vague conception of what "a harmony of structure and materials" might represent.

In the following year, Nelson Valjean wrote a first "true" biography of the writer, *John Steinbeck — The Errant Knight: An Intimate Biography of His California Years.* Valjean's book is in no sense a critical volume, yet as a reminiscence by yet another Steinbeck buddy, it is full of anecdotal value and charm. In another sense, though, it is like the work of many early critics of Steinbeck: it is rich in the knowledge of the California years, but it cannot accommodate movement. It is no disservice to Valjean to state that many of Steinbeck's early critics could not abide Steinbeck's leaving California.

Yet Valjean's title admits to his understanding of Steinbeck's identification with Arthurian themes, and also his sense of place. True to his stated mission, the biographer takes about three-quarters of his space and time just reaching the point of Steinbeck's first publications; and his lore is full of local-color referents. Valjean has little patience for the post-California years; Steinbeck's second marriage takes but a few pages to come and go; and his third is followed by his death in but two. Valjean can hardly wait to get John Steinbeck home:

> Now John's ashes are buried beside his ancestors in the oak-shaded Salinas Garden of Memories. It is a quiet cemetery. Fremont's Peak rises in the east, and to the west, not far away, are the weathered sandstone castles of Corral de Tierra, surely still peopled with the gallant knights of old. (Valjean 184)

Just as surely, no biographer has been at greater pains and haste to get his subject safely interred in what he feels to be Steinbeck's native literal metaphorical soil than Valjean. Valjean's study remains of interest even if, or because, its focus is — not necessarily defensively — on Steinbeck as a local boy.

In the same year, 1975, Richard Astro and marine biologist Joel Hedgpeth edited *Steinbeck and the Sea,* the papers delivered at Oregon State University's Marine Science Center in Newport. Not only is this volume scarce, but its seven essays are brief ones; yet we are introduced here to Steinbeck's biographer Jackson J. Benson, and treated to a spirited defense of Steinbeck by Astro himself, who rightly takes offense at the condescending obituary of the writer by, of all persons, Harry Thornton Moore (Astro/Hedgpeth 5).

Joel Hedgpeth's scant contribution seems to convey the same response to the land — and the sea — that Steve Crouch's photo-essay volume did. Consider Hedgpeth's short introduction to his own brief presentation:

> . . . In the summer, such towns [as Salinas] were hot, dry and somnolent. Salinas, however, was only a few miles from the sea, open to the cooling summer fogs with their smell of the sea. There were, of course, many hot and dusty days nevertheless, as it may have been when John rode his pony down the unpaved street near his home . . . (Astro and Hedgpeth 9)

What may be of importance here is the immediacy that bridges the worlds of photographer, marine biologist, and novelist — all were inspired by the same landscape.

Warren French was quick — as early as 1975 — to revise his 1961 TUSAS series volume and to do so extensively. Few critics have shown so much willingness to reconsider their views as French. As he confesses in his preface, "This fresh study might most suitably be titled 'Steinbeck and the Drama of Consciousness'" (French II 9). French admits to having borrowed his key critical rubric from scholars in pursuit of such subjects as Henry James (and, at the end of the study, Willa Cather), and this seems to enable him to hold on as long as possible to a term describing Steinbeck as a "naturalist," which is both an intriguing strategy and possibly also a fatal mistake.

French continues to harp at Peter Lisca (131), but he has clearly sidestepped his earlier commitment to *The Pearl*, which now "provides the kind of introduction that is a disservice to both its author — who wrote much better, controlled works — and to fiction itself by failing to suggest the tough-minded complexity of the greatest examples of the art" (130).

One must return in the end to French's new configuration of Steinbeck as a dramatist of consciousness. Ultimately, he finds that such a work as the final *The Winter of Our Discontent* fails because "Steinbeck's failures as examples of a penchant for moralizing" cause him "to lose touch with the senses" (168). French was finding new ways of dealing with the old topic of naturalism. French's phrase is not only telling, but also memorable. French noted at the time, and with respect to the writing of *Travels with Charley*, that Steinbeck himself seemed to have felt towards the end of his writing career that he had been out of touch with his audience:

> Steinbeck's undeniable "decline" as an artist almost surely resulted from a confusion of the multiple forms that "criticism" may take. The journalist deplores, or more rarely commends, specific present actions. The artist, however, is not a reporter, but a magician who conjures up a new world that provides us with a perspective for examining ours. A serious artist is not a tactical, but a strategic, critic; he is concerned not with specific happenings but with universal tendencies. This kind of artist Steinbeck was when he wrote in *Cannery Row,* "What can it profit a man to gain the whole world and to come to his property with a gastric ulcer, a blown prostate, and bifocals?" (19–20)

Well, there is precious little (to this date) to be done about bifocals or, for that matter, about Steinbeck's fixation on his critics; but French's own usage is of enduring interest: words like "reporter" and "magician"; and his professional employment of such map-room terms as "tactical" and "strategic." Warren French's 1975 revision comes to us replete with references not only to Steinbeck's favorite motifs, but also — in a sense— to French's own form of battlefield maneuvers.

In 1976, Richard Astro was back with a pamphlet, *Edward F. Ricketts,* curiously like the Gray title for Minnesota in 1971, at least in physical appearance. Boise State University's Western Writers Series needed to include Edward Ricketts, and Richard Astro was happy to oblige, apparently off the top of his head given his prior book. Steinbeck of course comes up repeatedly, but the interested scholar will want to peruse Astro's earlier volume instead of dabbling in these matters only scantily covered here.

In 1978, Peter Lisca weighed in with *John Steinbeck: Nature and Myth*, a thoroughgoing and new treatment of his earlier approach to the writer. Although it is not a series title, it is clearly a reflection on Lisca's first book. In fact, it answers the series (and its detractors) by deliberately reinventing the topics that serve as rubrics for chapters that are more or less chronological surveys, beginning with one that is bare-bones biographical. This time around Lisca, his subtitle notwithstanding, almost stints on philosophy, and his coverage of separate books is almost skimpy. Given the fact that Lisca was writing for a trade publisher this time around (Crowell), he played a safe hand; there is little if anything to challenge in his "nature and myth" coverage, and one notes that the intended audience is a younger one.

Lisca prefers instead to separate the nonfiction from the fiction; and he is perhaps the first and only critic of John Steinbeck to have noted that as the writer turned increasingly towards journalism in his later years, he also became more and more depressed, with *America and Americans* being "the most depressing book he ever wrote" (Lisca, *Nature* 235).

This could be fair if Lisca had meant it as only a parting shot at a writer, who, after all, had been putting food on many of our tables for many years — including Lisca's. Yet Lisca rises to the occasion when, in his final paragraph, he places Steinbeck in context:

> His real accomplishments are his eighteen volumes of fiction, and upon these his reputation rests secure. Among contemporary American novelists only William Faulkner approaches Steinbeck's variety of form and prose style. The range of Steinbeck's themes and subject matter is similarly impressive. Furthermore, he was able to achieve these things without losing the common touch. His ability to bring together in his novels and in his image of man both the scientifically described world and that of the intuition and imagination, nature and myth, without distorting either, that is Steinbeck's own unique genius. (236)

Lisca's second round with Steinbeck shows what can happen when a graduate student evolves into an independent-minded critic.

In 1978, Anne-Marie Schmitz published a limited-print volume called *In Search of Steinbeck*, a study of the various California homes Steinbeck and his wives had inhabited during the 1930s and 1940s. A beautifully presented book with color plates, its commentary is critically negligible.

In 1978 and 1979 there also appeared the two volumes of *The Outer Shores*, edited by Joel Hedgpeth from the papers of Ed Ricketts, and with the help of Richard Astro but largely based on Ricketts's scientific observations off the Pacific coast, with or without Steinbeck as a presence. To be sure, this is specialized material meant for the reader fascinated enough by Astro's book to want to follow it right through his pamphlet to Hedgpeth's volumes, but it is also a rich mine of information inaccessible elsewhere, and it is endowed with a number of rare illustrations, both photographic and cartographic.

Paul McCarthy produced another general-reader survey, *John Steinbeck*, for the Frederick Ungar Modern Literature Monographs series (in 1978). Lacking illustrations and breaking no new ground, McCarthy's book is primarily a library shelf-stuffer; in fact, it relies rather heavily on Nelson Valjean's bare-bones biography and some of the earliest and most basic critical writing. McCarthy's book is so anxious to stay on safe turf that one almost longs for the most feisty and adrenaline-raising language of a Howard Levant.

McCarthy is by no means a Steinbeck specialist, and his treatment of the writer's life and works makes no attempt to break new ground. Rather than extend the still-limited coverage the later works had received to date, McCarthy spends more than half his space getting Steinbeck past *The Grapes of Wrath*. To be fair, he has by that time also included a biographical essay, but even that skims through Steinbeck's life at a pretty fast clip. McCarthy manages to repeat a major gaffe within a pair of pages: he has the writer marrying "dancer Gwen Verdon" in 1943, and divorcing her for Elaine Scott just over five years later, that is, by the time McCarthy's p.17 has just become p. 19.

Two more volumes of real worth appeared at the end of the 1970s: the first attempt at a full biography of Steinbeck, Thomas Kiernan's *The Intricate Music: A Biography of John Steinbeck*, and Thomas Fensch's *Steinbeck and Covici: The Story of a Friendship*. Kiernan's book was not well received by Steinbeck specialists, who were well aware that a definitive and presumably authorized biography by Jackson J. Benson had been long in the works. Elaine Steinbeck, the writer's widow, helped Kiernan only "indirectly" (Kiernan xvii); and indeed there is little in the way of significant detail revealed by Kiernan, who seems to have written out of a fan's regard.

Kiernan's skimpy final chapter (308–15) seems to dismiss everything Steinbeck wrote after *Pippin*; in fact, the coverage of Steinbeck's last years is hardly adequate, whatever Kiernan thinks of the later output. To put things more bluntly, almost two thirds of Kiernan's book consists of relatively familiar information and takes Steinbeck only about three titles into his canon. There would seem to have been a problem with the biographer's ability to sustain his attention span throughout this flawed volume.

But to be fair to Kiernan, his account of Steinbeck's life is rich in anecdotal lore that may have resulted from personal interviews or from letters. It is thus something of a disappointment that his energies did not sustain themselves into a period from which he might have come up with even more firsthand accounts. Yet he is all too accepting of the received wisdom of the earlier Steinbeck critics, and bafflingly so, as one instance will show:

> Although not his last book, *East of Eden* was the climax of Steinbeck's artistic life, and a sad climax it was indeed. The book was published in the early fall of 1952 while he and Elaine were still in Europe. Although it did well commercially, Viking Press promoted it as John's masterwork and the serious critics proceeded to treat it with rough condescension. The consensus was that John had clearly reached the end of the creative road and was a writer whose value lay only in the books of his long-distant past. The best that could be said about it was that it was a noble allegory that didn't work. The reason was that Steinbeck, although he continued to write effectively evocative physical description, had lost his talent for characterization. (300)

When one turns to the footnote to this very paragraph, one learns that the "novel is today treated as something of a classic" (323) — making the reader wonder when such summary assessments are Kiernan's and when they are someone else's.

Steinbeck and Covici is a book that had to be done sooner or later. Thomas Fensch is by profession a journalism teacher and one should not turn to him for anything but honest facts — certainly not for daringly original criticism. Fensch wants to get down a clear record of a relationship in letters between editor and writer that spanned the years from 1937 to 1964, when the senior Covici died. Some critics may complain that Covici was too much the accepting business partner to have been of genuine worth in helping Steinbeck discriminate between his more valuable and riskier projects; and there is certainly no doubt that many a project, especially in the later years, miscarried. But as Fensch comments,

> The relationship between John Steinbeck and Pascal Covici, which previously had been cordial and mutually appreciative, began to be

> extremely warm and intimate. Covici worried about Steinbeck's pro-
> ductivity and pace, with a concern not just for a widely read and prof-
> itable author but for Steinbeck as a friend. Steinbeck, too, worked
> closely with Covici; he kept Covici well informed with the progress of
> his manuscripts, as well as his thoughts on a variety of subjects
> (Fensch, *Covici* 23)

That is putting things mildly; Steinbeck at times seems to be writing as intimately to Covici as though he were talking to himself.

That leaves Fensch with a problem — either to get between the two men somehow at some loss to his own objectivity or to withdraw modestly while performing a neutrally editorial function. Happily, he chose the latter role. That is not to say that Fensch would not be an interesting commentator on Steinbeck's writing, on Covici's role as editor, or on the literary implications of the relationship between the two — a relationship in which frequently a great deal hung in the balance. What Fensch's book manages to accomplish — besides adding another Steinbeck title to the canon — is to let his readers argue that the two men drew out the best in one another's professional characters and made the rest of us the richer for having done so. *Steinbeck and Covici* reminds us of what good journalism is all about, even in this era of media-driven "hype." It means not standing in front of your story, and this Fensch has not done.

All in all, the 1970s were a most productive decade. Steinbeck studies were off and running, with serious and even competitive scholarship going on, and there was less and less need for the defensive apologetics of the 1940s. Even Steinbeck's partial detractors were proving, through their attentions, that he was deeper than they had suspected, that his readership was justified in their tastes, and that there was much more work to be done. A crucial part of that work will be examined in the following chapter.

Works Consulted

Astro, Richard. *Edward F. Ricketts*. Boise, ID: Boise State U, 1976.

————, *John Steinbeck and Edward F. Ricketts: The Shaping of a Novelist*. Minneapolis: U Minnesota P, 1973.

————, and Joel W. Hedgpeth, eds. *Steinbeck and the Sea*. Corvallis: Oregon State UP, 1975.

Burrows, Michael. *John Steinbeck and His Films*. St. Austell, UK: Primestyle, 1971.

Covici, Pascal, ed. *The Portable Steinbeck*. New York: Viking, 1971.

Crouch, Steve. *Steinbeck Country*. Palo Alto, CA: American West, 1973.

Davis, Robert Murray, ed. *Steinbeck: A Collection of Critical Essays*. Englewood Cliffs, NJ: Prentice-Hall, 1972.

Donohue, Agnes McNeill. *A Casebook on "The Grapes of Wrath."* New York: Crowell, 1968.

Fensch, Thomas. *Steinbeck and Covici: The Story of a Friendship*. Middlebury, VT: Eriksson, 1979.

French, Warren. *Filmguide to "The Grapes of Wrath.*: Bloomington: Indiana U P, 1973.

————, *John Steinbeck*, rev. ed. Boston: Twayne, 1975.

Gale, Robert L. *Barron's Simplified Approach to Steinbeck: "Grapes of Wrath."* Woodbury, NY: Barron's, 1967.

Gray, James. *John Steinbeck*. Minneapolis: U Minnesota P, 1971.

Hedgpeth, Joel W., ed, *The Outer Shores,* Parts One and Two. Eureka, CA: Mad River Press, 1978 and 1979.

Kiernan, Thomas. *The Intricate Music: A Biography of John Steinbeck*. Boston: Little, Brown, 1979.

Levant, Howard. *The Novels of John Steinbeck: A Critical Study*. Columbia: U Missouri P, 1974.

Lisca, Peter, *John Steinbeck: Nature and Myth*. New York: Crowell, 1978.

————, ed. *John Steinbeck: "The Grapes of Wrath": Text and Criticism*. New York: Viking, 1972.

Marks, Lester Jay. *Thematic Design in the Novels of John Steinbeck*. The Hague: Mouton, 1969.

McCarthy, Paul. *John Steinbeck*. New York: Ungar, 1980.

O'Connor, Richard. *John Steinbeck*. New York: McGraw-Hill, 1970.

Pratt, John Clark. *John Steinbeck*. Grand Rapids, MI: Eerdmans, 1970.

Schmitz, Anne-Marie. *In Search of Steinbeck*. Los Altos, CA: Hermes, 1978.

Valjean, Nelson. *John Steinbeck: The Errant Knight*. San Francisco: Chronicle, 1975.

3: Tetsumaro Hayashi
and the Steinbeck Society

THE LATE PRESTON BEYER, an eastern American book dealer and bibliophile, and Tetsumaro ("Ted") Hayashi, a Japanese-American academic most of whose career was spent at Ball State University in Muncie, Indiana, founded the John Steinbeck Society in 1966. Two years later, Hayashi changed what had been a *Newsletter* (a more recent *Steinbeck Newsletter* has been published under very different auspices at San Jose State University, California) from a mimeographed periodical into a printed Quarterly. In fact, a journal dependent on the energies of (for the most part) a single if highly committed individual could never have become a true quarterly in practice, and *The Steinbeck Quarterly* never did.

What it could become, and did until late 1993 or thereabouts, was a semi-annual publication that had a lasting impact on Steinbeck studies for a quarter of a century; locus or focus for the activities of the International John Steinbeck Society, which has already hosted four Congresses around the world; and sponsor of the Steinbeck Monograph Series, an annual of enormous impact on the international Steinbeck community. Quite likely there has been nothing like it in the name of any other American author. Hayashi made the world of Steinbeck studies considerably more available, particularly to younger critics. The present writer was once one of those; I was in effect lured away from study of other writers by Hayashi's insistent offers of this or that publishing opportunity. In turn, he and his readers were always eager to give fair consideration to what were, in effect, seminar papers written by graduate students; it is somewhat thrilling to hear one's own former student quoted by an unsuspecting senior scholar halfway around the world.

In 1971 Richard Astro edited, with the help of Tetsumaro Hayashi, the proceedings of the first important Steinbeck conference ever held, co-sponsored by Ball State University in Muncie and Oregon State University in Corvallis. What was most remarkable about this 1970 event is that it brought together the leading lights of the first generation of Steinbeck critics, the new names from the second, and the surviving members of the Steinbeck-Ricketts scientific coterie.

Steinbeck: The Man and His Work (1971) is a splendidly edited account of a memorable conference held at a university hitherto known mostly as the venue for Bernard Malamud's classic novel of academe at its most bucolic, *A New Life*. Photo-illustrated but containing only ten papers as chapters, it is in its economy and resilience a model for future such ventures — and still a pleasure to hold in the hand. One might single out Robert DeMott's paper, "Steinbeck and the Creative Process: First Manifesto to End the Bringdown Against *Sweet Thursday*," not only to praise it but for its prophecy. The title ironically reflects an era coming to a close — an outer world heretofore off-limits to the hermetic kingdom of "name" critics — and foretells of a new way of seeing the later Steinbeck: as a proto-postmodernist.

It was also DeMott who began to name the group of scholars who, after Corvallis, began to show up at one Steinbeck panel or conference after another the "Steinbeck Roadies." A most congenial group — though hardly uncompetitive or lacking in frankness — this movable feast of critics (and often their spouses) seemed genuinely to enjoy one another's company, and to nourish themselves on one another's work, over the next quarter-century and more, not excepting social occasions. (At the Tuscaloosa conference long after, for instance, one evening ended in some fairly energetic dancing.)

The formal welcome by Tetsumaro Hayashi that leads off the volume (Astro and Hayashi v-viii), is essentially a promotional "plug" for the new John Steinbeck Society. To this end, it should be remembered that on the occasion of this first conference of its kind, Steinbeck himself had been dead for less than two years, and his Society barely operational as yet. The ten contributors reflect the past, present, and future of Steinbeck scholarship; names of achieved distinction include Charles Shively writing about Steinbeck's notion of community, James P. Degnan on Steinbeck's war against California's land monopolies, Robert M. Benton on *Cannery Row* and ecology, and Charles R. Metzger writing about Mexican-American figures in Steinbeck.

Peter Lisca was on hand with a study of Steinbeck's contrasting types of protagonists, and Robert Morsberger showed the fruits of his work on the *Viva Zapata!* script. Along with DeMott's prophetic essay, already mentioned, I contributed an expanded version of a Steinbeck-Faulkner comparison which in an overlapping form had appeared in an early *Steinbeck Quarterly,* with both in turn being based on my doctoral dissertation — which Hayashi had been quick to sleuth out the existence of, thus sending this then-young writer on his unsuspecting way to a lifetime of work on Steinbeck.

Besides Astro's balanced introduction, there is an essay by the aforementioned marine-biologist Joel W. Hedgpeth, and a "reminiscence" by Steinbeck's longtime pal Webster ("Toby") Street, a Monterey lawyer who shows up touchingly, in disguise, in *The Acts of King Arthur and His Noble Knights*. Street's rambling but invaluable presentation was a special treat for all present, as is clear in this candid excerpt from his final paragraph:

> I don't really know anything about literary criticism, but I have a lot of ideas about it, and if I had the time I would probably put them in print. But coming back to this question of the soil, I was convinced that while John was writing about the people and places he knew, he was writing very well; but when he left California and started to make it up, as in *Burning Bright*, he fell apart. (41)

Just as William Faulkner suffered the grumbling of a lawyer friend (Phil Stone), so had Steinbeck. Toby Street likely felt Steinbeck had deserted his old ties in abandoning a changed California. One might note that the early Steinbeck had done a fair amount of writing about "people and places" he did *not* know, but made up; but to many of his California buddies from the early years, Steinbeck's moving east meant betrayal of them and their place, where they had chosen to stay. One has to sympathize with the provincial Street, who lets "soil" trap him in the (local) ditch of saying, in effect, I don't know anything about art, but I know what I like. Or like what I know.

Such an observation only adds to the wonderful variety and permanent value of Astro and Hayashi's pacesetting volume.

Because this chapter occupies a central and overlapping position in this survey, its uniqueness argues a certain autonomy of format, since it extends itself over three decades of scholarship. It begins with the published proceedings of a pioneering Steinbeck conference Hayashi helped bring about; it speaks of Hayashi's first book-length Steinbeck bibliographies; it deals with the several items in the Steinbeck Monograph series; it considers the four items in the short-lived Steinbeck Essay Series; and it concludes by covering seven books bearing Hayashi's name, the last of which contains the proceedings of an important Steinbeck Congress. A comparison of the tone and contents of the two conference volumes which in effect bookend this chapter would in itself be a measure of what took place in the twenty-year interim.

Hayashi's name appears on a good many publications, though he himself was less often an original critic than a scholar and a driving force. One of his earliest projects was the publication in 1973, through

Scarecrow Press, of *A New Steinbeck Bibliography*, a listing of works by and about John Steinbeck running from the earliest days through about 1971. Inclusions are numbered, and the volume is a great time-saver for students. A second volume was issued in 1983, covering the years from 1971 to 1981. And a younger scholar, Michael J. Meyer, has prepared a supplement running through to the late 1990s, also published by the same firm. Meyer's work has been careful, and his edition stronger, more sensibly organized, and easier to use than its predecessors. It also benefits from a more easily read typeface. In spite of its seemingly hefty price, it is a must volume for serious libraries and individual scholars, especially those who are writing dissertations. It should be noted that at least in the first two bibliographies, there are some obvious errors in data and also certain duplicate entries; nonetheless, Hayashi's contribution was unprecedented and unparalleled.

Unfortunately, the scope of this volume prohibits my covering the valuable materials presented by the *Steinbeck Quarterly* over the years. It is also regrettable that only samplings of the two decades of titles from the Steinbeck Monograph Series list can be offered here; but this is, after all, a book about books. Perhaps at a future date the best of the SMS entries can be gathered together in hardcover format, for by now many of them are becoming increasingly scarce.

Appropriately, the series began in 1971 with *John Steinbeck: A Guide to the Doctoral Dissertations*, a survey going back to the 1940s and often consisting of wholly new, commissioned redactions. The list of contributors is by now a curiosity, containing as it does names of scholars who have continued to be prominent in Steinbeck studies as well as many who simply went on to other work. Hindsight suggests that Hayashi might well have usefully included Master's degree theses from the same era, but that would have made for too thick a publication.

The second SMS title was by Creighton University Professor Reloy Garcia: *Steinbeck and D. H. Lawrence: Fictive Voices and the Ethical Imperative*. That Steinbeck and Lawrence were in effect kindred spirits had long been taken for granted but this had not been seriously explored as an area of criticism. Garcia readies his detailed comparison of the two men's works and careers with this initial presentation:

> Far beyond . . . general similarities, Steinbeck and Lawrence tilled further common ground: while both saw themselves as moral activists, both were also compelled to withhold their commitments to society; both were pressed to voice moral anguish, but both were tempted to withdraw into the relative security of nature, or primitivism, or history, or even into the unthorned world of myth and symbol. It is this

ambivalence, this evolving conflict between the public man and the private person, this conflict between social and political immersion, and an opposing inclination to withdraw, that shapes their work and which governs their esthetic distance; further, it provides a rhythmic dialectic just beneath the surface of their fiction and drama. (Garcia 5)

Garcia thereby brings similarities of style and subject back to matters of fundamental temperament.

Marston LaFrance edited the third SMS volume when its author, Lawrence William Jones, was untimely killed in a traffic accident in England. If Jones had been able to complete it, *John Steinbeck as Fabulist* would have taken Steinbeck studies off in a new direction a decade earlier than actually became the case. Jones's conclusion contains a useful caution to the generation that would outlive him:

> Even if one does grant the fabulist his latitude, however, it remains difficult to give one's assent, even when reading parables, to a concept of evil which entails merely some form of withdrawal or separation from the communal wholeness of life. To students of American literature this concept has the ominously familiar ring of Emerson; for while Steinbeck was able to formulate a distinct vision of good for human life, he was unable to formulate a correspondingly distinct vision of evil; ultimately he offers merely a stipulative vision of it as a lack of unity or community. (Jones 32)

Thus, and not without precedent, Jones places Steinbeck "in the literary tradition deriving from Emerson as opposed to that deriving from Hawthorne and Melville" (32).

This is a crucial issue, and it has not yet been convincingly dealt with. Steinbeck wrestles with the matter in his later fictions, and seems to very much want to embrace the notion of personal badness and culpability, as the alternative to the amoral objectivism he had inherited from Ed Ricketts and never quite shaken off. Steinbeck lets the Ricketts character Jim Casy in *The Grapes of Wrath* argue that it is futile to make moral judgments of human actions. But Steinbeck never believed that, and the writer of fiction can never, dislike him as you will, subscribe entirely to Ed Ricketts's notions.

The fourth SMS title anticipates, in effect, this present one. Hayashi himself edited *Steinbeck Criticism: A Review of Book-Length Studies* (1974), and to be accurate, it is a review of reviews — some reprinted original responses and some commissioned especially for the monograph, seventeen in all — and surveys the most significant critical titles already mentioned in this text. Because individual contributions are often evaluative as well as descriptive, the interested reader may want to seek out Hayashi's text and compare it with this one.

SMS No. 5 is another collection of essays edited by Hayashi, *Steinbeck and the Arthurian Theme* (1975). Only four essays are included — French's on Steinbeck and Malory; Arthur F. Kinney's on *Tortilla Flat*; and two by independent English scholar Roy S. Simmonds on Steinbeck's late-life project, the modernization of Malory's *Morte d'Arthur*, which only in the following year would be published as *The Acts of King Arthur and His Noble Knights*. Kinney's essay goes beyond the usual simplistic assumptions that because Steinbeck drew attention to the Arthurian parallels in *Tortilla Flat*, they were either merely satirical or probably unsophisticated. Kinney uses the novel's *paisanos* to make an ironic commentary on the larger, respectable society and its corrupting influence on even the theoretically simple and innocent:

> The *comitatus* is their chief ritual, but there are others: the sharing of grappa, the privacy of sexual affairs, the pretense to morality and guilt (as in burning down Danny's house). Their counter-culture is reinforced through their joint attack on the capitalistic society which surrounds them and which, in its advocacy of property and its insistence on unalterable responsibility, challenges them with its own enduring vitality. But what the Christian communism of the *paisanos* masks is their own capitalistic proclivity. It is not true, finally, that the *paisanos* combat capitalism or absorb its ways unknowingly; what we come to learn is that they actively embrace it. . . . (Hayashi, *Arthurian* 19)

Thus Hayashi's slender anthology was also a preview of coming attractions; and the introduction is by myth-scholar Joseph Fontenrose. Hayashi contributes a useful selected bibliography.

The annual series continued in 1976 with an extended essay entirely by Simmonds, by now establishing himself as a Steinbeck scholar of international reputation. In its mere forty pages, Simmonds's monograph manages to provide a fair assessment of *Steinbeck's Literary Achievement*. Not without his own strong opinions, Simmonds provides Steinbeck with a rationale for the experimentation that led readers of his postwar writing to dismiss it. Simmonds quotes Steinbeck's *Eden* journal to the effect that "A good writer always works at the impossible," and appends his own observation by way of conclusion:

> If Steinbeck was guilty of anything at all, it was certainly not of prostituting his art, but rather of immense artistic courage. He was never content to rest on his laurels, as he might easily have done, by continuing to reproduce what he had already demonstrated he could

do supremely well. Had he steered the safe, well-tried course, it is just possible that he may have been a greater writer in the last analysis, if not, because of his unpredictability, such an exciting one. (Simmonds, *Achievement* 39)

And Simmonds concludes by rounding off his real theme, that John Steinbeck must be judged in the context of major writers in English, particularly American ones:

> Steinbeck's work is firmly established in the mainstream of traditional American literature, the mainstream formed in part from the three converging streams of transcendentalism, vernacularism, and regionalism, in each one of which the undying vestiges of Old World literary traditions are still very much alive. There is, for all his endless (but, in one sense, limited) experimentation with style and subject matter, a quality of intrinsic and reassuring classical simplicity about Steinbeck's work. He learned his lessons well from the old masters. It is this quality which endows his books with their aura of enduring stability, timelessness even, so that in the long run, one can speculate with some assurance, his work will date neither as rapidly nor with such finality as the work of some of his more stylistically daring and currently more highly regarded contemporaries. (39–40)

Currently being revised and expanded, this essay is a model of its kind. For all its brevity, Simmonds's monograph is a succinct analysis of lasting value.

By now probably almost impossible to obtain is a mimeographed monograph commemorating the 1976 "Bicentennial Steinbeck Seminar" jointly cosponsored by Ball State and Taylor Universities on the Taylor campus in Upland, Indiana, on May, 1 1976. French and Hayashi were on hand, to be sure, but the event was certainly on a small scale and of little scope. *Steinbeck's Prophetic Vision of America*, edited by Hayashi and Kenneth D. Swan, is not a publication fully worth the trouble of seeking out.

The author of this present text contributed the next year's (1977's) monograph, *Essays on "East of Eden."* A set of three interrelated pieces, it was the first attempt to give sustained coverage to Steinbeck's second "big" novel on its own, and in a time when the book was still routinely dismissed. The essays carry on the Simmonds suggestion that we respect Steinbeck's willingness to innovate (with attendant risk) and discuss the notion of "East" in the book, the author's use of nature to index character, and his experimentation with narrative voice in a postmodern, reflexive mode.

In this monograph, I made suggestions that are derived from my doctoral dissertation. In a second section entitled "Outside of Paradise: Men and the Land in *East of Eden*" I addressed that dissertation's major theme:

> For John Steinbeck as much as for certain other American writers of fiction — such as William Faulkner, Willa Cather, and Robert Penn Warren — the relationship of individual characters to something which (for want of a more specific term) can be called "Nature" becomes the index of their individual worth, the graphs on which their human development — or lack of it — can be traced. It is this correspondence between Nature and "virtue" (in the older sense of the word) to which I now intend to give consideration at some length, for I believe that in *East of Eden* Steinbeck attained a height of sophistication in the usage of this device which he consistently used throughout his novelistic career. (Ditsky, *Essays* 15)

This notion of Nature as an index of the individual worth of characters is in fact, as said above, the gist of my doctoral dissertation, which considers all of Steinbeck, along with Faulkner and Cather. In hitting upon a measure of human worth that runs through Steinbeck's writing from beginning to end — do you exploit Nature or make right use of it; do you treat the land as a food source or as real estate? — this chapter hits upon a means of ultimately defending Steinbeck's "other" great novel by coming to terms with its candidly patent intentions and methodology.

Michael J. Meyer is currently working on a book-length study of things "oriental" in Steinbeck, a vast subject that of course is a major reason for Steinbeck's enduring popularity among Asian readers of foreign writing. In the third essay of my monograph, entitled "The 'East' in *East of Eden*," I tried to justify the presence of the Solomonic servant Lee, adviser to the novel's characters and source of much exasperation to the novel's critics:

> Lee may, as a character, spring from Steinbeck's earlier conception of Orientals as mysterious personages, but he can hardly be described by that platitudinous racial epithet *inscrutable*. Indeed, the highly Americanized and articulate Lee is nothing if not scrutable: he is a *raisonneur* figure who does much of the novel's explaining. He is as present to the novel's central characters (though invisible to their racist neighbors) as he is removed from direct participation in its main events. He observes, and he comments, and he moves the action along. If he displays the protective guise of the "tomming" American black, a matter of using the words and gestures that the unthinking

expect of your ethnic group, he is also a puller of strings who organizes scenes with the careful orchestration of a tea ceremony. (48)

Lee as a character is, then, a walking explanation of what Asian readers "see" in Steinbeck's writing.

As for my first section, it was my first effort — perhaps the first effort by anyone — to take as anything but a defect in style and structure Steinbeck's use of multiple voices, including that of an intrusive narrator. As I say of Steinbeck's presence in *East of Eden*:

> . . . Relentless experimenter, he fused together multiple styles, that of his expository prose (the commentator-voice that introduces sections, generalizes, and creates contexts); the similar voice that is used to recount the saga of the Hamiltons (and which begins to surface as an "I" — though one still contained in "we" — only near the end, when a Steinbeck only slightly younger than himself recalls a season he had shared, co-existed in, with his scarcely-elders, Cal and Aron Trask); and the elevated, rather mannered, even somewhat theatrical, expressionistic voice of much of the Trask material . . . (13–14)

Evidently, if there is a unity to my trilogy of essays it is Steinbeck who provides it.

In 1978, Hayashi, Yasuo Hashiguchi and Richard F. Peterson edited *John Steinbeck: East and West*, papers presented at the First International Steinbeck Congress held at Kyushu University in Fukuoka in the late summer of 1976. Except for the repetition of my essay from a part of my monograph of the year before, SMS No. 8 is with two exceptions the work of Japanese critics (that is, if one excludes Hayashi himself). The small American contingent present felt itself a part of a valuable initial exchange of ideas with their Japanese colleagues, the core of an Asian contingent that at future congresses would be supplemented by members from India, Korea, Thailand, and China. Warren French, unable to attend, provides an objective overview to a seemingly disparate parliament of viewpoints in which scholars who had now been interacting for over twenty years were introduced constructively to one another's thinking.

Coverage of these titles is necessarily foreshortened by reason of the scarcity of many of these texts; but the serious scholar will find means of laying hands on them. A pioneering venture (for its time, 1979) is Hayashi's edition of *Steinbeck's Women*, SMS No. 9. On the one hand, the feminist at the millennium's end is likely to find these essays insufficiently theoretical; on the other hand, they (five of the six are by women) are honest readings of Steinbeck's often conflicted presentation of female nature, a viewpoint that is objective yet also studded with be-wilderment, or at least fascination.

The sole male presence, Robert E. Morsberger, weighs in with an essay entitled "Steinbeck's Happy Hookers," which taps into the ten-dency Steinbeck shared with many an American male writer — that is, to sentimentalize (with the conspicuous exception of *Eden*'s Cathy Trask) prostitutes. The pieces by women critics are more interested in portrayals of ungeneralized, individual characters. It is interesting to note that four of the essays are by women recently drawn to Steinbeck studies: Mimi Reisel Gladstein, and Sandra Beatty, a graduate student at the University of Windsor in Ontario. It is to Hayashi's credit that he not only accepted Beatty's seminar paper but also commissioned her second, for a Modern Language Association Convention panel; Hayashi had always searched for and employed new talent.

Marilyn L. Mitchell has not been an active Steinbeck scholar since this publication, Sandra Beatty has long since given herself to high-school teaching and administration, and Morsberger's specialized inter-ests in film have led him to broader topics. But this SMS number intro-duced many who might not have seen her work in the *Steinbeck Quarterly* to Mimi Reisel Gladstein, an academic whose brand of femi-nist thinking finally pulled criticism of Steinbeck's work regarding fe-male characterizations into the late twentieth century. Gladstein gets the last words in the monograph, and we might well give time to con-sidering them here. She is speaking of Juana, the long-suffering wife of Kino in *The Pearl:*

> Juana is a composite of all the best qualities of the archetypal feminine. But for all her positive characteristics, Juana remains a flat character. As Woman she is nurturing and indestructible. As the sym-bol for womanhood she functions in admirable and beneficial ways, but as an individual woman, one Juana, wife of Kino, her personality never takes shape. As representative of her positive values, her pres-ence presages affirmative future possibilities. A general criticism of Steinbeck has been the paucity of female characters in his works. While this is true, one must not ignore the significance of those who are there. Juana in *The Pearl* is a case in point. (Hayashi, *Women* 52)

One must not miss Gladstein's point here: to the extent that men, in-cluding writers, think of women as "indestructible," they place them on a pedestal and, if even in positive and well-meant ways, stereotype them and are thence free to wipe their hands of them as individuals.

In 1980 the indefatigable Hayashi edited SMS No. 10, *Steinbeck's Travel Literature*; and when one stops to think about the topic, it seems inescapable that Steinbeck is a writer who, more than most, tallies with the great American theme of Americans in restless motion, a kind of Brownian movement of the spirit that preoccupies Steinbeck from his first title to his last. And that of course includes both fiction and nonfiction.

In fact, *Steinbeck's Travel Literature* was originally intended to include just about all of the latter and *Grapes* among the former. As things turned out, *Cup of Gold* is covered, along with *The Wayward Bus*, and there are two essays apiece on *America and Americans* and *Travels with Charley*. Familiar names appear here (Simmonds, Astro, Betty L. Perez, and Richard F. Petersen) along with those less so (Darlene Eddy, Charles J. Clancy). Astro's opening essay is the most ambitious in scope:

> If a work of travel literature is to be of lasting value, it must reflect the kind of curiosity which leads to discovery and thence to knowledge. Implicit in the pattern of reality shaped by the mind of the writer in the *Log* is the clear relationship between travel and knowledge, between voyage and discovery. But Steinbeck's writings about his travels through two wars are the work of a mentally muscle-bound writer whose behavior reflects first the impetuous rush to arms in the name of the national interest, followed by a constriction of the whole picture in the name of the war effort which have come to define so well the responses by too many Americans to things military. (Hayashi, *Travel* 6–7)

Fair enough, for an essay originally printed in the year the Vietnam War ended. But note how accommodating Astro can be to a later volume essentially recording a series of disappointments:

> *Travels with Charley* is a superbly honest volume. In it, the novelist puts his life on the line and in so doing makes himself anything but a passive figure in a cohesive structure of feeling. In the end, Steinbeck's change of scene led to a change of heart by a writer who had written about America for years with hope and finally with a deep sense of pain and anguish. (10)

This engages our interest. Steinbeck, who had literally put "his life on the line" in two wars, captures our respect most when, presumably, he does so metaphorically.

One year later, Hayashi was back with *A Handbook for Steinbeck Collectors, Librarians, and Scholars* — specialist material, to be sure, but one with a surprising number of interested collectors involved. There are tributes to such major Steinbeck collectors and dealers as Adrian

Goldstone by Preston Beyer, Maurice Dunbar, and Lee Richard Hayman, themselves writing about their collecting careers; sadly, Beyer himself has recently died, and tributes to his own humaneness have been coming in from all quarters of the Steinbeck bibliographic cosmos he so long represented. As his passing reminds us, SMS No. 11 is specialist coverage necessarily dated by now, particularly in the subsequent surveys of individual library holdings which have of course grown in the interim, particularly the Steinbeck Research Center at San Jose State University (now the Martha H. Cox Center for Steinbeck Studies; Cox was the Center's founder). Visitors to the Center today will find a warmly comfortable place to work with an extensive collection — including many unique items.

With this publication, Hayashi announced that the SMS could no longer appear as an annual issue, but would instead become an "occasional" one. Indeed, not until 1986 did a twelfth number appear, Hayashi's own *John Steinbeck and the Vietnam War (Part I)*. (There would be no Part II, because Steinbeck's estate objected to the dissemination of matter that might be taken as harmful to the writer's reputation, though Steinbeck's position was less advocacy of the war than of the ideals of the American soldiers who fought in it.) Hayashi's coverage is therefore limited to what had been before fairly public knowledge, including the Long Island journal *Newsday* in which Steinbeck's "Letters to Alicia" appeared, 1965–67. But he also considers the once-famous print controversy between Steinbeck and Soviet poet Yevgeny Yevtushenko, in which Yevtushenko took Steinbeck to task for seemingly deserting his proletarian principles. Aside from what is the "Japanese" habit of numbering entries instead of providing more transitional language (scarcely a mortal sin), Hayashi's coverage holds up well as a report on the last war Steinbeck reported on.

That coverage is as balanced as Steinbeck might have wished for. He pays attention to the war situation as Lyndon B. Johnson inherited it and as it flared up in (or at) his hands. Steinbeck's patriotism was always premised on loyalty to the dog-soldier, the unwilling battlefield presence in all wars, and he would therefore not brook any besmirching of the motivations of the common G.I. We might well attend Hayashi's final summation:

> His partisan involvement in the Vietnam War — especially during the Americanization of the Vietnam War — revealed John Steinbeck defending Lyndon B. Johnson, who "was determined to be a leader of war *and* peace and who failed in both desperate endeavors. Johnson once referred to "that bitch of a war" and wished that he could

"concentrate on the woman I really loved, my cherished Great Society." Thus Steinbeck, like President Johnson, had to experience the Vietnam War as "a personal as well as a national tragedy." (Hayashi, *War* 17)

This seems apt, but for the rest of us, only the full release of the war-related materials will let us go beyond the most simplistic of judgments about an event in history over which so many of us, one way or another, eventually caught our judgments nodding.

Only three more titles remained to be published in SMS. Hayashi and Thomas J. Moore edited Steinbeck's *"The Red Pony": Essays in Criticism*, SMS No. 13, for release in 1988. It is a return to the briefer sort of monographs of the early days of SMS, and it consists of one essay apiece devoted to the four final chapters of *The Red Pony*. Three are of the close-reading, traditional sort, and these concern the last three sections, "The Promise," "The Great Mountains," and "The Leader of the People"; and they are handled by critics by then established names and voices in Steinbeck studies: Robert S. Hughes, Jr., Roy S. Simmonds, and Mimi Gladstein. Once again, Warren French provides the introduction, and he rightly notes that the initial contribution, Thomas M. Tammaro's "Erik Erikson Meets John Steinbeck: Psychological Development in 'The Gift'," is, or was then, the sort that "would more likely turn up in a journal devoted to popular culture or the relationships between literature and psychology" (Hayashi and Moore, *Pony* xiv). Quite true; but few might have predicted in 1988, if not only how much more the latter area of interest would continue to grow, that it would be the bandwagon of "cultural studies" at many a university.

French concludes of Tammaro's essay that it is "perhaps more stimulating in raising more issues than it settles." And that "[such] criticism suggests the wide variety of future directions in which the study of *The Red Pony* may proceed in testifying to the universal vitality of this legend of a young man's coming of age in the early twentieth century in a remote valley of California and the continuing inspiration it provides for coming to terms with the defeats and triumphs of human experience" (xiv). It is hard to tell whether French is trying to predict the future of Steinbeck studies here, or simply throwing his hands up at seeing such a cross-cultural, multidisciplinary approach as Thom Tammaro's. Increasingly and inevitably, Steinbeck studies — like so many others — have had to accommodate to a progressive broadening of theoretical and varietal approaches to a once seemingly "tame" subject.

Steinbeck's Posthumous Work: Essays in Criticism (No. 14 in the SMS sequence, 1989) contains only five (new) essays, with an introduction by longtime standby critic Reloy Garcia: Nancy Zane on *Journal of a Novel*; John H. Timmerman on *Steinbeck: A Life in Letters*; Clifford Lewis on the screenplay *Viva Zapata!*; Michael Sundermeier on *The Acts of King Arthur and His Noble Knights*; and Maurice Dunbar on *Letters to Elizabeth* (Otis, Steinbeck's longtime agent). Many of these names we have already encountered; the rest we will meet shortly. Predictably, the essays are somewhat uneven in quality and scope but the slim volume is well worth perusing. It, too, was coedited by longtime Hayashi associate Thomas J. Moore.

A particularly thorny subject is tackled by Clifford Lewis in his essay "Outfoxed: Writing *Viva Zapata!*," which considers the interference in the film project by Twentieth Century Fox's producer, Darryl Zanuck, and director Elia Kazan. Lewis has always been astute at dealing with topics related to politics, and it is hard to disagree with his final evaluation that

> . . . Steinbeck's original version remains forceful enough to have withstood the cheap tricks added to the film along the way. To a modern audience unfamiliar with internal and external totalitarian threats to democracy in the early 1950s, *Viva Zapata!* addresses different issues. It speaks of a great man who fights to retain a pastoral culture, who places the community above self-interest, and who challenges the validity of progress. . . . (Hayashi and Moore, *Posthumous*, 33)

This monograph is particularly uneven both in content and style, but it was the result of an idea long overdue.

A year shy of the nineteenth anniversary of John Steinbeck's birth, the Steinbeck Monograph Series came to an end with SMS No. 15, Hayashi's edition of *Steinbeck's Short Stories* in *"The Long Valley": Essays in Criticism* (1991). The stories are covered, one essay per story, in the order in which they appear in the original collection, and there is a final essay by Robert S. Hughes, Jr., who was currently becoming a leading specialist in Steinbeck's short fiction (along with John H. Timmerman). Warren French again provides the introduction, showing how, from his unique perspective, each essay either fulfills its mandate or could and should have gone further. A new voice, Patricia M. Mandia, is heard from, writing on "Johnny Bear" and "The Murder." Robert M. Benton, a more familiar figure, discusses "Flight" and "The Snake"; and Thom Tammaro handles the maverick pig fable "Saint Katy the Virgin." The suddenly prominent Louis Owens takes on "The Harness" and the perhaps deliberately as regards character stereotyped "The Vigilante." An eager Michael J. Meyer is given "Breakfast," "The White

Quail," and "The Raid" (with its echoes of a section of *In Dubious Battle*. Susan Shillinglaw takes on Steinbeck's more frequently anthologized story, and one that is enduringly problematical, "The Chrysanthemums." Shillinglaw would go on to take over the San Jose Steinbeck Research Center and eventually start publishing what was originally known as *The Steinbeck Newsletter*, which not only replaced the *Steinbeck Quarterly* but, unlike the journal, drew upon a wider range of reader, anecdotal, historical, and generally non-specialist materials, as well as the ample illustrative materials available within the archives of the Center.

Shillinglaw's own essay deftly contrasts Steinbeck's use of the Pygmalion myth with those of Ovid and Shaw, and concludes:

> Steinbeck's treatment of the Pygmalion legend is thus much bleaker than either Ovid's or Shaw's, both of which, however different, end in self-assertion. As she exits, Elisa Allen cries not because she is yet weak or old, but because she is defeated by the bourgeois vision she must accept as her own. Ironically, the water that the land and the farmers so eagerly await at the beginning of the story arrives at last: tears of death, however, not of life. (Hayashi, *Stories* 8)

Shillinglaw cannot have hoped to do full justice to what is perhaps Steinbeck's most frequently anthologized story in her brief piece, but applying the Pygmalion myth to "The Chrysanthemums" is a strategy both fresh and apt.

Because they cover such a vast range of themes, there is no way to avoid backtracking in trying to cover all of Tetsumaro Hayashi's projects; this seems the appropriate place to mention the volume that SMS No. 15 was intended to update but not replace, and to indicate new, worthwhile directions for criticism and scholarship. We are referring to *A Study Guide to Steinbeck's "The Long Valley,"* published by The Pierian Press in Ann Arbor in 1976.

There would seem to have been no harm in our having discussed SMS No. 15 before its predecessor, because the later work complements but in no real sense supplants the earlier essay collection. True enough, some of the same critics were aboard, such as Benton (but discussing different stories); and the anthology again concludes with a general essay (by Brian Barbour) on "Steinbeck as a Short Story Writer." But not all the critics included were the "big name" ones (Lisca, French, Fontenrose, et al.). And it is interesting to note that the only female critic is Bob Morsberger's wife, Katharine — perhaps indeed a sign of quainter times. Though the book is lengthened by the inclusion of the four *Red Pony* chapters, it is, in spite of its ostensibly greater length, a volume that consists of markedly shorter pieces than its successor, something made the clearer when one notes that the (often skimpy) annotation and the accompanying discussion questions are printed in the same large type as the texts. In short — and this is not to challenge the validity of its contents in general — this book was and is truly meant for high school readers and not really for the university-level students it pretends to address. Thus each volume has its own value and its own audience, and neither is quite wholly able to claim precedence over the other.

Interestingly, Barbour's overall treatment of the stories in *The Long Valley* appears at the end, rather than the beginning, of the volume. It alone is unaccompanied by elementary study questions, though like the rest of the text it is weakened by a Dick-and-Jane typeface and typographical errors. Barbour is a tough reader of Steinbeck's short fiction:

> . . . Fiction, I believe, was a means for Steinbeck to focus and release his very generous humanity. In this respect the diffuseness of the novel served him better than the more disciplined shorter form. The short story has no room for hollow notes. It must sound true wherever it is tested (being, in this respect, closer to poetry), its whole life has to be expressed in every passage. I do not think Steinbeck took the measure of the short story art form, and I believe his abandonment of the form without such mastery hastened his involvement and preoccupation with fabular fictional forms in his later writing. (Hayashi, *Guide* 126)

This is a teasing conclusion to an anthology of criticism, and one cannot help but wonder what a next paragraph might have said. Is a reputed master of the short-story form to be rated the weaker because he switched to other and longer forms? Or do those "fabular fictional forms" somehow imbibe the energies of a misspent initial vocation?

There is more. Just as the SMS was waning, Hayashi began a modestly-conceived "Essay Series," the first title of which was published in 1986 as *Steinbeck's World War II Fiction, "The Moon Is Down": Three Explications.* That they are, to be sure; but as Reloy Garcia notes in his introduction, these three papers on the same work, largely conceived of as conference papers, are also "complementary" in nature. Hayashi has written about the play-novella's political dimension, the dramatic function of the character Dr. Winter, and — finally — the Shakespearean implications of the referents in Steinbeck's text. (Here, Hayashi is clearly onto a subject that deserves a study of its own spanning the entirety of Steinbeck's canon.) Modestly conceived and brought forth, this first Essay Series volume (1986) is plastic-spiral bound and has the look (if not the substance) of a graduate-student paper of the era. But by now it is probably so scarce that it would have to be, in some way, special-ordered for new scholarly use.

Hayashi's essay on Shakespearean referents is in fact a falling-back on professional strengths, since his primary teaching area has been not Steinbeck but Renaissance drama. That suggests something that might initially seem ironic about a play-novella that also appeared as a short novel. Garcia puts a finger on a salient difference between the two versions of *The Moon Is Down* when he observes, in his introduction, that

> . . . the best approaches to the work . . . are literary ones, approaches which, while marveling at its social and psychological complexities, find it lacking in characterization, for example, or scope. Bluntly, I think the novella had a big enough problem, for a novel, something Steinbeck apparently didn't recognize. That is why, I believe, it makes a more satisfactory play than a novella; the play, fuller bodied, partially compensates for what the novella lacks. (Hayashi, *War* 3–4)

In other words, Steinbeck's portentous dialogue, oversized characters, and melodramatic action (particularly relying on "offstage" business and implication) are greatly redeemed by the visual "reality" of a stage production, where there is no denying that what is seen and heard of and from the actors is "actually" happening. A reader of the play-novella — and Hayashi's essays in response to it might even conclude that what influenced Steinbeck the most in the writing of *Moon* might have been the radio drama of the era.

Similarly bound and in the same copied-typescript format of the time, and therefore suitable for treatment at this point, is Hayashi's *A Student's Guide to Steinbeck's Literature: Primary and Secondary Sources*, like the title above disseminated under the auspices of Ball State University's Steinbeck Research Institute. Now of course badly dated, this brief title is also difficult to find, pitched too high in its title, and pitched too low in its intended audience. Nowadays, an undergraduate would bring up this much information by computer in a matter of moments. Well-intentioned, this is a short manual only a librarian with the right budget would seek out today.

The second item in the Steinbeck Essay Series, *John Steinbeck on Writing*, adopts the formatting of the *Steinbeck Quarterly*. This time, Hayashi has compiled a large number of comments on the craft of writing from previously available Steinbeck titles, nearly all from non-fiction sources (journals, letters, etc.). These appear as numbered and topically entitled paragraphs within six arbitrarily chosen but sensible rubrics: "Advice on Writing"; "The Craft of Writing"; "A Novelist as a

Minstrel" (brief but engaging); "Work Habits"; "Censorship"; and "Literature, Journalism, and Criticism." Hayashi has appended an essay on "The Art and Craft of Writing" as regards Steinbeck. There is an overly brief introduction, again by Garcia. In the end, one finds nothing really new in this anthology, but it is useful to have these quotations assembled under one roof, so to speak; and one can readily imagine a student writing a paper by applying these statements to a single title and testing their validity as realized in practice (or not).

Largely a convenience for the reader primarily interested in Steinbeck's major work, Hayashi assembled in *Steinbeck's "The Grapes of Wrath": Essays in Criticism* (1990) what he considers the eight finest essays on the novel to have appeared in the *Steinbeck Quarterly* in the 1970s and 1980s. Of particular interest is the fact that by no means all of the contributors are truly Steinbeck specialists; and so their readings bring to bear insights garnered elsewhere. Even the brief introduction by John H. Timmerman makes patent use of his recent research into Steinbeck's short fiction, relating relatively unknown early writing to the later masterpiece. The collection may provide a useful shortcut for hurried student scholars.

We have space for but a single example of the original insights contained in this anthology that, for all its reduplications of essays to be found in earlier issues of the *Steinbeck Quarterly*, does bring together in one convenient location an interesting and varied set of responses to Steinbeck's major work. Not only does this make it a useful setting for comparing the essays' various approaches, but it simplifies matters for the scholar — or library — who did not subscribe to the more than two decades of *SQ*.

As for that single example: Helen Lojek contributes an essay entitled "Jim Casy: Politico of the New Jerusalem"; it places Casy firmly in a tradition he is often assumed to have simply abandoned:

> This mingling of social criticism with a continued faith that some form of New Jerusalem is still possible places *The Grapes of Wrath*, firmly in a tradition which Sacvan Bercovitch finds deeply rooted in American literature. The ritual of the jeremiad or fast-day sermon, as it was adopted to American circumstances, Bercovitch explains, has so shaped the American consciousness that "American writers have tended to see themselves as outcasts and isolates, prophets crying in the wilderness. . . . *American* Jeremiahs, simultaneously lamenting a declension and celebrating a national dream." The country's failure to live up to its early promise is not a reason to despair, but a reason for people to reaffirm that early promise and rededicate themselves to it.

Steinbeck's double vision of California — his rage at its denial of the American dream of the New Canaan and his conviction that the migrants may yet make that dream a reality — yields a twentieth-century resurgence of the jeremiad's simultaneous lament and celebration. (Hayashi, *Grapes* 54–55)

Lojek concludes that Casy's "change from religion to politics . . . is indicated by Casy's persistence in the evangelist's habits of thought and rhetoric . . ." Lojek has managed to retain Jim Casy as a member of an honorable American tradition, rather than as a mere lapsed believer.

The Steinbeck Essay Series came to an end with a fourth volume, a reprinting of an essay by Steinbeck's biographer, Jackson J. Benson. Benson's piece had originally appeared in a 1977 issue of *Western American Literature*; the original title, "John Steinbeck's *Cannery Row*: A Reconsideration," was retained for the monograph, and of course it makes for a fairly short volume. It is not clear why Hayashi decided that an article that had been so recently published in so widely read a journal should be reprinted, but there is no denying that it deserved even wider dissemination than it had had originally. Benson brings his biographical skills and research lore to bear on a novel that had been looked at largely as some sort of amusing quirk in Steinbeck's writing career. He places the work where it belongs, as a point of departure for Steinbeck, as well as an attempt to do something for a friend who "could not write very well." He places *Row* in the context of *Sea of Cortez*:

> *Sea of Cortez* came out to mixed reviews and did not sell very well. Perhaps it was this lack of interest in the nonfiction narrative which led Steinbeck only two years later to what amounted to using the more comfortable novel form to fictionalize the basic material of *The Log*. By this time, also, I rather suspect that the power of Ricketts' philosophy resulted in large part from Ricketts' unique personality. So the problem for Steinbeck the writer became how to get this man that he loved so dearly down on paper whole and intact. (Benson, *"Row"* 26–27)

One need not wholeheartedly agree with this assessment of the novel's function in Steinbeck's own career in order to see it as a fitting summation of Steinbeck studies to this point.

But there is more — seven whole books, in fact. Like Benson, Hayashi was for years also interested in the work of Ernest Hemingway; and in 1980 he followed through on the mission chosen for the first SMS number by expanding its scope and its subject matter with *Steinbeck and Hemingway: Dissertation Abstracts and Research Opportunities*

(1980). Note the subtitle: Hayashi's unique force as an editor lay not merely in his ability to delegate duties, but especially to suggest to others, particularly young scholars, directions worth pursuing. Thus Hayashi's career, however self-motivated, must be seen as what he would characteristically say (of others) in Steinbeck terms, that is, he was a "leader of the people."

In fairness to the designated apostle this time around, scholar Richard F. Peterson, it must be noted that he provided the chapters on "Research Opportunities" for both writers. At the same time, it must be admitted that these "opportunities" consist largely of an analysis premised on a survey of the included abstracts, that is, the analyses are meant to provide a sense of where Steinbeck and Hemingway studies had been going to date, and not to concoct and give away free original notions. French again provides the introduction, a justifiable polemic on the problems facing incipient scholars at the time. Although a single thorough index appears at the end, this is in great part two volumes in one; and, to no great surprise, the Hemingway section is roughly twice the size of the Steinbeck one. And just as this book is an updating and expansion of the Steinbeck material in one of the earliest monographs, so it too is by now nearly two decades old and so in need of updating that it hardly can be said to reflect new trends in criticism anymore.

Steinbeck studies were also served by the next five volumes to be considered, a duet and then a trio. In 1973, Hayashi published (again with Scarecrow Press of Metuchen, New Jersey), the first volume of *Steinbeck's Literary Dimension: A Guide to Comparative Studies.* The subtitle's intended meaning is itself double: the book means to survey studies of Steinbeck's work in contrast and comparison, stylistic and philosophical, to some eleven other writers, some of whom may come as an initial surprise to readers. These writers include putative influences on Steinbeck or interesting parallels, perhaps resulting from similar creative or historical circumstances. Of course, Hayashi appends a survey of recent trends in Steinbeck criticism. Peter Lisca also contributes an essay that provides a summary of Steinbeck criticism to date, an effort resembling the present one but also including key essays; Lisca's tone is fair and positive.

There is insufficient space to deal with all individual inclusions, but it is informative simply to read the list of authors certain critics found comparable to Steinbeck: Dickens, Faulkner, Hemingway, Kazantzakis, Lawrence, Mainwaring, Milton, Salinger, Adlai Stevenson, Penn Warren, and Zola. Surely this is as disparate an assemblage as could be imagined in Steinbeck's company.

John L. Gribben, for example, takes on the seemingly unlikely coupling of Steinbeck and John Milton. But his focus is most sensible, basing itself on the issue of free will in both authors, especially as embodied in the *timshel* ("Thou mayest") motif that is crucial to the Trask portion of *East of Eden*. Of this aspect of *Eden*, Gribben makes this comparative remark about Milton:

> In *Paradise Lost* Milton asserted the same freedom for man, illustrating his thesis with another basic story, the story of Adam and Eve and their fall. Theology in Milton's day had muddled the issue of human freedom, balancing the freedom of man against the foreknowledge of God, and finding man to be not so free as he had thought he was. Milton's prime concern was to justify God's ways to man, but much of his justification involved establishing the man whose mind God "hinder'd not Satan to attempt" as a man "with strength entire, and free will armed." (Hayashi, *Dimension I* 96–97)

Thus Steinbeck takes the issue of a creating God who made Adam and Eve knowing full well they would (and must) transgress, and brings it to the next generation, where God makes human options clearer rather than issuing commands. In so doing, Steinbeck has in effect taken on the problem posed most excruciatingly by the Book of Job.

Or, to choose another instance, Andreas K. Poulakidas uses socialism as the ultimate wedge between the visions of Steinbeck and Nikos Kazantzakis:

> . . . However much his characters suffer — and if this could be measured, I would venture to say that Steinbeck's characters are made to suffer more than Kazantzakis' — Steinbeck's social realism is a provincial one, a chauvinistic, non-idealistic one. (64)

So that this volume's "voices from without" serve a special and unique purpose in offering original talking points to readers and critics whose primary prior focus might have been Steinbeck seen in isolation.

Eighteen years later, a much more sophisticated version of Scarecrow Press issued *Steinbeck's Literary Dimension: Series II*; new topics this time involve Hardy, Blake, Jung, William March, Charles G. Norris, Mark Twain — and Ed Ricketts. There is a second but very different essay involving Faulkner, and no fewer than four on Hemingway. Indeed, Jack Benson's contribution is characterized by an impressively apt title: "Hemingway the Hunter and Steinbeck the Farmer." Benson makes a point-by-point comparison of the two writers in biographical, career, and thematic terms. He notes that Steinbeck, unlike Hemingway, "was not a very competitive man, and his relations with nature

were based on a desire to understand and cooperate with the environment rather than dominate it." Further,

> If Hemingway played the part of Deerslayer, the white hunter,
> then Steinbeck played Chingachgook, the native American who felt a
> kinship with nature. In his suffering, the Hemingway protagonist tells
> us, humanity is important; in Steinbeck's work humanity is but a
> speck in a very large universe . . . (Hayashi, *Dimension II* 56)

Benson, in his penultimate paragraph, summarizes his views of the two
writers as constituting archetypal American values:

> Steinbeck suggested to us that we can either husband our resources,
> maintain an intimate relationship with the earth and its creatures, and
> learn to care for each other in time of need, or we perish in our blind
> egotism, our selfish competitiveness, our self-hatreds. Steinbeck the
> farmer. Hemingway suggested that we must learn to master our envi-
> ronment, compete successfully in the arenas of society and nature, and
> have the courage to face alone the certain hardships that living entails,
> or we can be victimized by our surroundings, be forced to surrender
> our freedom and lose our individual identities, and be enslaved by our
> fears and illusions. Hemingway the hunter. (61)

Nearly fifteen years later, Benson's essay seems all the more timely, rec-
ognizing as it does — for better or worse — that these two writers
"would seem to have embodied the fundamental values of the American character" — as he notes in concluding a few lines later.

A delightfully crabby introduction to this Series II title is (again)
provided by Garcia, who is eager to defend Steinbeck against trendy de-
contructionists. It might be noted that if any author needed decon-
structing, Steinbeck would have beaten the critic to the punch. This
pair of volumes reinforces the tired professor's suggestion to his or her
students that the readiest route to an "original" paper lies in comparative studies, where no one else is likely to have ventured. Thus this series winds down being at the service of the graduate students Hayashi
was always so fond of fostering.

In 1974, Hayashi launched a different series of book-length studies.
Indeed, he called them "Study Guides," though they are far superior in
coverage and complexity to any hack-writer's manual for a student harried by a deadline. It does not seem to have been intended that these
essays break new ground; instead, they are sound and solid readings
provided by some of the most renowned of Steinbeck critics (Lisca, Astro, French, and so on).

This first volume, *A Study Guidebook to Steinbeck: A Handbook to His Major Works*, subsequently in effect Part I, was meant to focus on the acknowledgedly major works, including nonfiction titles — though not all readers, and for that matter even the contributors, would necessarily agree with the choices for inclusion, such as *America and Americans* and *The Winter of Our Discontent*. There are separate essays on *Of Mice and Men* in both its play and novella form; and Robert Morsberger is on hand with a piece on "Steinbeck on Screen." An oddity about the trilogy, as it eventually became, is that the works covered appear in alphabetical order, as if to deliberately interrupt any expectation of chronological flow and, perhaps, inhibiting unwarranted consistency of vision.

Warren French provides a tantalizing short foreword — a matter of not even four pages —that considers Steinbeck under the rubric "The Artist as Magician." In it, he professes to wish to engage teachers and students in an honest, unprejudiced reading of a writer who never balked at being popular as well as serious. As he notes of Steinbeck, "It is clear that he looked upon his characters as people, on himself as creating and populating a world, as a magician — in short — not soberly reflecting back the world around him with mirrors, but conjuring up a different world" (Hayashi, *Study* xv). This is more than valid; it is a concise rejoinder to a generation of critics who insisted on reading Steinbeck as just another 1930s realist, and who as a result went about either figuratively beating their foreheads or trying, in print, to punish the writer.

A Study Guide to Steinbeck (Part II), 1979, goes methodically about the business of tying up loose ends, considering as it does just about everything deliberately left out of Part I. Thus by implication its coverage extends to lesser works, in which case it shows *East of Eden* poised for promotion. The contributors again include Morsberger, Roy S. Simmonds, Charles J. Clancy, Richard F. Peterson, and Martha Heasley Cox; each person has written two essays on different topics, making it possible to compare individuals' approaches to more than one title as well as to one another. However, the format precludes daringly original approaches. As with its predecessor, Part II is outfitted, chapter-by-chapter, with each book's background, plot synopsis, a basic critical explication, a bibliography, and questions for research pursuit. There is also a lengthy catechism of questions and answers mostly intended to tout the activities of (and membership in) the now-defunct Steinbeck Society, a certifiably dated aspect of a volume that nevertheless has no real peers.

An example of this anthology's relative sophistication is this summary judgment (by Robert Morsberger) of a salient aspect of *The Wayward Bus*, which Morsberger says is Steinbeck's

> ... first prolonged attempt to study sexuality seriously and explore the complexity behind the stereotypes. The novel deals with lust more than with love ... Sex of this sort amounts to little more than animal magnetism, with Steinbeck's natural man and woman "doing what comes naturally." There are other, more sensitive and substantial possibilities than this, or macho seductions, or marriage as only a trap. But at least *The Wayward Bus* challenges the cheap exploitation of sex and makes us think about more honest and meaningful relationships between men and women. (Hayashi, *Study II* 227)

Morsberger's summation, suggesting that the novel's presentation of sexuality is laden with irony, is, when combined with the remembrance of what was going on in the writer's life at this time, the clue to a possibly quite profound and original study of an often disparaged work. But in accepting the book's chosen format while refusing to "write down" to its putative readership, this and other included essays show an honorable critical adulthood very willing to welcome worthy candidates to admission.

This series too came to a close, and in 1993, with *A New Study Guide to Steinbeck's Major Works, With Critical Explications*. This incredibly clumsy, or should we say "uncatchy," title is nonetheless precise enough, unless we wish to quarrel with its inclusions and, therefore, designations. The previous format has been retained, but by now Scarecrow had caught up with the times and was issuing attractively printed texts. Essays contributed by Helen Lojek and Charlotte Hadella represent relative newcomers to Steinbeck country; but there are also a pair apiece by major new voices: Barbara Heavilin, Michael J. Meyer, Patrick W. Shaw, and especially Louis Owens — whose distinctive point of view we shall survey later.

The format is consistent with its predecessors, and Hayashi included material gleaned from his monograph on Steinbeck and the writer's craft. What is perhaps of at least momentary interest is the editor's reduction, or at any rate redaction, of what the major Steinbeck works were or are. There are only ten chapters dealing with specific titles one at a time, and these include *America and Americans, Cannery Row, East of Eden, The Grapes of Wrath, In Dubious Battle, Of Mice and Men, The Pearl, The Red Pony, Travels with Charley*, and *The Winter of Our Discontent*. This is a list designed, unintentionally, to annoy many while enraging a few.

What is in effect Hayashi's "last hurrah" as an editor is his edition of the North American papers delivered at the memorable Third International Steinbeck Congress held in Honolulu in 1990. The superbly produced volume from the University of Alabama Press appeared in 1993. Honolulu appeared to be a happy meeting place for Japanese and other Eastern scholars with North Americans, as might well be imagined; and the essays collected in *John Steinbeck: The Years of Greatness, 1936–1939* prove to be a happy blend of what had become the second generation of Steinbeck critics with a smattering of a third. John Timmerman provides the introduction to a set of essays that quite naturally break down into two categories well suited to the venue. I lead off with a study of the women in *The Long Valley* and their conflicted sexuality; the subtitle, "Steinbeck's Elusive Woman," suggests that the author himself found womanhood baffling for much of his life. The poems Steinbeck wrote for his second wife, Gwyn, became an evocative presentation for Robert DeMott. Abby Werlock and Charlotte Cook Hadella look at key female characters in *In Dubious Battle* and *Of Mice and Men*.

Hadella's essay, "The Dialogic Tension in Steinbeck's Portrayal of Curley's Wife," is in its treatment of *Of Mice and Men* an example of the clear arrival on the Steinbeck scene of a new generation of readers no longer content with close readings, but anxious to apply literary theory to his works. Perhaps Hayashi's volumes of comparative studies had a bearing on this phenomenon, but it is patent enough that not only had previous approaches largely done their work — leaving, seemingly, not that much to be said — but also that the new generation had come from an academic world now dominated (some would say "ridden") by theoretical approaches.

Hadella immediately explains her title:

> For the term "dialogic tension," I am borrowing from Mikhail Bakhtin's theory of discourse as dialogue between a speaker and a listener, about a hero or subject. In the rhetorical triangle of speaker-listener-subject, Bakhtin substitutes "hero" for "subject" and views hero as active agent, interacting with the speaker "to shape language and determine form. At times, the hero becomes the dominant influence in written utterance." Dialogic tension exists in all discourse because words, the elements of the dialogue, are loaded with various social nuances that influence each other and perhaps even change as a result of the association. (Hayashi, *Greatness* 65)

One wonders what "Toby" Street would have had to say about all this. Indeed, one wonders what Steinbeck himself might have had to say by way of response.

The second part of this anthology, again without apparent advance planning, dealt neatly with what would thenceforth be called "Steinbeck's Worker Trilogy." Essays are contributed by Shillinglaw, Morsberger, Fensch, Gladstein, Tammaro, and Owens. Though it appears in the second section of the anthology, Louis Owens's essay on the Filipino fictionist Carlos Bulosan leads ingeniously into a discussion of the worker novels, and to the question of why existent Californian minorities of the era were not included in Steinbeck's coverage. It is fitting that the editor has placed Owens's piece, in fact, directly after Hadella's, for he also makes use of Bakhtin's notions, producing yet another example of new directions in Steinbeck studies. For instance, he speaks of *In Dubious Battle's* character Mac recycling a phrase he had previously used to describe the dead character Joy to the effect that "He didn't want nothing for himself":

> . . . When Mac repeats the same words about Jim, Mac is in dialogue with himself, and in repetition his words have taken on a hint of what Bakhtin calls "authoritative discourse," or "privileged language" that approaches us from without. The result is a double-voiced utterance that appears to unite, within Mac, both "the authority of discourse and its internal persuasiveness." This hybridization is introduced by the introductory epithet of "Comrades"; the word arrives with the full weight of authoritative discourse behind it. This is what Bakhtin calls a "prior discourse," one that bears an authority "already acknowledged in the past." Between introductory epithet and double-voiced utterance, through Mac's and the novel's last words, Steinbeck — perhaps America's unsurpassed master of what Bakhtin defined as dialogism in the novel — has brilliantly highlighted the irresolvable tensions embodied in the work. (88–89)

New approaches, but not any longer in tight unanimity, were on display at this enormously successful Congress. The overall rubric under which the principals operated is a debatable one — even to those who were present — but the outcome is certain enough. Participants brought to Hawaii particularly strong arguments, a sure sign of a genuine resurgence in a newly-confident era of Steinbeck scholarship. Notes are, oddly but not inconveniently, all tucked off to the end of the volume.

For someone like this writer who has received as many as three separate messages from Ted Hayashi on three separate subjects on the same day, this chapter documents activity that may not strike ordinary persons as extraordinary, but the *extent* of this chapter is surely evidence that Tetsumaro Hayashi has been a tsunami in Steinbeck Studies. Nearly all of the critics who appear in these pages have been touched by his presence, whether or not they have been active members of the Steinbeck Society or contributed to its publications. We resume our survey in the 1980s, where it will be clear that enormous changes had occurred in Steinbeck criticism.

Works Consulted

Astro, Richard, and Tetsumaro Hayashi, eds. *Steinbeck: The Man and His Work.* Corvallis: Oregon State UP, 1971.

Benson, Jackson J. *Steinbeck's "Cannery Row": A Reconsideration.* Muncie, IN: Steinbeck Essay Series No. 4, 1991.

Ditsky, John. *Essays on "East of Eden."* Muncie, IN: Steinbeck Monograph Series No. 7, 1977.

Garcia, Reloy. *Steinbeck and D. H. Lawrence: Fictive Voices and the Ethical Imperative.* Muncie, IN: Steinbeck Monograph Series No. 2, 1972.

Hayashi, Tetsumaro, *John Steinbeck and the Vietnam War (Part I).* Muncie, IN: Steinbeck Monograph Series No. 12, 1986.

———, *A New Steinbeck Bibliography, 1929–1971.* Metuchen, NJ: Scarecrow, 1973.

———, *A New Steinbeck Bibliography, 1971–1981.* Metuchen, NJ: Scarecrow, 1983.

———, *Steinbeck's World War II Fiction, "The Moon Is Down": Three Explications.* Muncie, IN: Steinbeck Essay Series No. 1, 1986.

———, *A Student's Guide to Steinbeck's Literature: Primary and Secondary Sources.* Muncie, IN: Steinbeck Bibliography Series No. 1, 1986.

———, ed. *A Handbook for Steinbeck Collectors, Librarians, and Scholars.* Muncie, IN: Steinbeck Monograph Series No. 11, 1981.

———, ed. *John Steinbeck: A Guide to the Doctoral Dissertations.* Muncie, IN: Steinbeck Monograph Series No. 1, 1971.

———, ed. *John Steinbeck on Writing.* Muncie, IN: Steinbeck Essay Series No. 2, 1988.

———, ed. *John Steinbeck: The Years of Greatness, 1936–1939.* Tuscaloosa. U Alabama P, 1993.

———, ed. *A New Study Guide to Steinbeck's Major Works, with Critical Explications.* Metuchen, NJ: Scarecrow, 1993.

———, ed. *Steinbeck and the Arthurian Theme.* Muncie, IN: Steinbeck Monograph Series No. 5, 1975.

———, ed. *Steinbeck and Hemingway: Dissertation Abstracts and Research Opportunities.* Metuchen, NJ: Scarecrow, 1980.

———, ed. *Steinbeck Criticism: A Review of Book-Length Studies (1939–1973).* Muncie, IN: Steinbeck Monograph Series No. 4, 1974.

————, ed. *Steinbeck's Literary Dimension: A Guide to Comparative Studies.* Metuchen, NJ: Scarecrow, 1973.

————, ed. *Steinbeck's Literary Dimension: Series II.* Metuchen, NJ: Scarecrow, 1991.

————, ed. *Steinbeck's "The Grapes of Wrath": Essays in Criticism.* Muncie, IN: Steinbeck Essay Series No. 3, 1990.

————, ed. *Steinbeck's Short Stories in "The Long Valley": Essays in Criticism.* Muncie, IN: Steinbeck Monograph Series No. 15, 1991.

————, ed. *Steinbeck's Travel Literature.* Muncie, IN: Steinbeck Monograph Series No. 10, 1980.

————, ed. *Steinbeck's Women: Essays in Criticism.* Muncie, IN: Steinbeck Monograph Series No. 9, 1979.

————, ed. *A Study Guidebook to Steinbeck: A Handbook to His Major Works.* Metuchen, NJ: Scarecrow, 1974.

————, ed. *A Study Guidebook to Steinbeck (Part II).* Metuchen, NJ: Scarecrow, 1979.

————, ed. *A Study Guide to Steinbeck's "The Long Valley."* Ann Arbor, MI: Pierian, 1976.

————, Yasuo Hashiguchi, and Richard F. Peterson, eds. *John Steinbeck: East and West.* Muncie, IN: Steinbeck Monograph Series No. 8, 1978.

———— and Thomas J. Moore, eds. *Steinbeck's Posthumous Work: Essays in Criticism.* Muncie, IN: Steinbeck Monograph Series No. 14, 1989.

———— and Kenneth D. Swan, eds. *Steinbeck's Prophetic Vision of America.* Upland, IN: Taylor U P, 1976.

———— and Thomas J. Moore, eds. *Steinbeck's "The Red Pony": Essays in Criticism.* Muncie, IN: Steinbeck Monograph Series No. 13, 1988.

Jones, Lawrence William, ed. Marston LaFrance. *John Steinbeck as Fabulist.* Muncie, IN: Steinbeck Monograph Series No. 3, 1973.

Meyer, Michael, ed. *The Hayashi Steinbeck Bibliography, 1982–1996.* Lanham, MD: Scarecrow, 1998.

Simmonds, Roy S. *Steinbeck's Literary Achievement.* Muncie, IN: Steinbeck Monograph Series No. 6, 1976.

4: The 1980s: Revisions

Now OUR MORE OR LESS CHRONOLOGICAL JOURNEY can be resumed. Although there is some overlapping of effort from one decade to the next and no sharp delineation between critical methods employed, I will divide the remaining two chapters by the respective decades they will cover: the 1980s and the 1990s. I hope that when this book appears in the last year of this century, 2000, its contents will herald the critical developments in Steinbeck studies that the next decade, at least, will produce.

The world of critical thinking outside of Steinbeck studies as such was having an inevitable impact as younger scholars brought to bear the innovative theoretical tools they had learned to use, for better or worse, and Steinbeck — that perennially innovative author — was outfitted with new gear and made to look as though he were keeping up with the times, as if he had not been doing so all along.

Thus it seems roughly accurate to entitle these chapters for their revisions of older points of view (the 1980s) as well as for the new approaches attempted (the 1990s). But a salient feature of Steinbeck criticism to date — and there have been few exceptions to this insight's validity — is that his serious critics have always seemed open to revisionist thinking, even when it has required their backing off from the strongly held positions of the past.

A case along those lines could be made for the late Joseph Fontenrose who, two years shy of two decades after his important 1963 study *John Steinbeck,* published a limited-edition monograph called *Steinbeck's Unhappy Valley,* a study devoted wholly to *The Pastures of Heaven* and initially intended to be part of a longer study of short-story cycles. Fontenrose recognizes the book's uniquely brilliant presence among Steinbeck's first three published works:

> It is a surprisingly successful book as a work of creative fiction, although it attracted little attention before Steinbeck won general recognition three years later. . . . Of Steinbeck's first three books, *Pastures* is easily the best; it has the stature of his later fiction and was soon recognized for its true worth after Steinbeck had won fame as a novelist. (Fontenrose, *Unhappy* 2)

The reader may recall that Fontenrose was a myth-critic and an analyst of authorial philosophy who was profoundly skeptical about either system. When he deals with a purported "curse" in the "Pastures of Heaven" that according to rumor is the doing of a local family, the Munroes (who appear throughout the story sequence and seem in some way or another to affect each narrative's outcome negatively), he doubtless tallies Steinbeck's own authorial suspicions of such happenings:

> There are no ghosts and devils, and there is no curse. . . . The Munroes represent the reality, which defeats the dreams, and illusions of men. . . . There is no supernatural force at work. There are only the land, the people on it, and a menacing new world round about. . . (46–47)

In other words, Joseph Fontenrose seems the critic most attuned to the early, Ricketts-era John Steinbeck.

But Fontenrose had already established the fact that while the Munroes are no supernatural force, their presence is a crucial unifying device in the story sequence:

> Thus the Munroes affected every one of these residents alike, whatever the person's condition: he may be prosperous or poor, industrious or lazy, imaginative or without imagination, neurotic or healthy-minded, educated or ignorant, sociable or solitary, in any combination of these traits. Each story is so placed in the sequence as to set one combination of characteristics in correspondence and contrast with another set. (24)

Not all readers will accept Fontenrose's happy vision of a seemingly symmetrical "unhappy valley," but those who have ever visited the actual Corral de Tierra — between Monterey and Salinas — will understand how anyone encountering its castlelike outcroppings, particularly a John Steinbeck already infatuated with medieval romance, would find it a challenge to, and a stirring of, the imagination.

A year later, in 1982, there appeared another Prentice-Hall title, this one devoted entirely to *The Grapes of Wrath*: Robert Con Davis's *Twentieth Century Interpretations of "The Grapes of Wrath."* Consisting of previously published articles or chapters, Davis's anthology is of no original worth. Its dust jacket even mentions by name five of the writers in its first section, including Leonard Lutwack, French, and Lisca, and it promises "8 others."

Davis's own introduction is, however, of special interest. For instance, he notes Steinbeck's almost unique refusal — for his era — to endow objects with values beyond their actual and inherent, non-literary worth:

> . . . In virtually any sampling of American novels before 1939, physical objects signify the presence of complex fictional relationships.
>
> Steinbeck's car repair scene, on the other hand, like many other work scenes in *The Grapes of Wrath,* locks physical objects in a single position. The connecting rod does *not* signify a plurality of possible associations, and the dark crankcase oil has no associations at all except as engine lubricant. Associations different from these are abruptly foreclosed by the unusual militancy of the car repair process. Rather, the scene presents objects as nonfunctioning signifiers, broken meanings that assert a neutral resistance, one to be overcome and defined by the three men. By thus depicting objects so that they approximate a semblance of dull matter, with only their immediate use and function to define them, the scene presents a strictly mimetic vision of work as the transformation of material into usable goods. Objects in the scene create the neutral resistance of undone work, and the one-dimensional presentation of the scene shows men *bringing* meaning to the articles they touch, objects that speak only of clearly articulated human ends. (Davis, *Grapes* 8)

At the same time, Davis has noticed the sacramental character of work in Steinbeck's writing, one which derives from no authorial intrusion, but from the values his creations imbue it with.

There were four volumes of varying degrees of interest published in 1983. Photographer Tom Weber issued *Cannery Row: A Time to Remember.* There is hardly any text to speak of, and yet the photos, to bring back an old but useful cliché, "speak volumes" about a vanished era.

Brian St. Pierre published *John Steinbeck: The California Years,* an illustrated mini-biography based on the common premise that Steinbeck was at his best when he was "at home," in one of his many California homes. This neatly printed volume, part of a short series devoted to West Coast writers, seems especially illuminated by the author's knowledge of the space he writes about. Like Weber, St. Pierre was able to draw upon the oral documents that had begun to be accumulated in Salinas at what is now the new local Steinbeck center. St. Pierre shows a geographical bias. In St. Pierre's biography, Steinbeck is divorced from first wife Carol on one page, moves to New York with second wife Gwyn and writes *The Moon Is Down,* and three pages later he is dead. But St. Pierre has written his obituary, in effect, and dated it 1942:

> Although Steinbeck came back to Monterey and Salinas for ex-
> tended visits after World War II, and once fantasized about buying a
> ranch in the area, he never lived there again. He became something of
> a wanderer, an exile from his literary Eden; his writings about it then
> were, in the main, diffident, awkward, and clumsy. He had drawn his
> strength as an artist from his native soil and, like Antaeus of Greek
> myth, he had lost it when he left it. (St. Pierre 112)

For a writer whom his home town had long viewed with suspicion,
John Steinbeck had come a long way to be accused of losing his myth-
like status for leaving his native state. But this volume could not say
otherwise; it is part, after all, of a "Literary West Series," and its attitudes are those one encounters today at Steinbeck gatherings from San
Francisco and San Jose to Monterey and Salinas. The iconography of
the Californian Steinbeck even extends to the cover's borrowing of a
-local portrait of the writer, in jacket and sports shirt, as engraved for his
1979 American postage stamp. In spite of its admitted bias, this book is
a pleasure to hold and read, even though it in a sense was marking time
until a full biography could be issued.

Stoddard Martin published *California Writers: Jack London; John
Steinbeck; The Tough Guys* in 1983. (The latter category includes the
detective-fiction writers Dashiell Hammett, James M. Cain, and Raymond Chandler.) Authors such as Frank Norris are also included, and it
is informative to read about Steinbeck in the context of writers whom
readers in other parts of the country have perhaps seldom considered
together. There is an undeniable ruggedness to California fiction that
all these writers share.

Martin does not avoid regional chauvinism, and that sort of defen-
siveness seems endemic to Steinbeck studies from whatever region.
Martin wants to like *The Wayward Bus,* and his reading of the novel in
gender terms can seem persuasive indeed:

> . . . At base, Steinbeck's women seem to doubt their ability to find
> satisfactory men. His men, correspondingly, become disillusioned
> about their ability to find satisfactory women . . . Steinbeck was a
> fearful man in the realm of desire. He was confused about women be-
> cause he was confused about what he wanted for and of himself. Art
> was the natural place for this confusion to be worked out. (Martin
> 121)

But, Martin goes on to say, such "forced conclusions" as the one that
brings *East of Eden* to an end can seldom satisfy.

Arguably true. Yet Martin goes on to force a conclusion on his own
subject: "For this reason Steinbeck's career once he left his native valley

failed, albeit in a most informative way, to live up to its original promise" (121–22). Many have made similar claims about Steinbeck's work; but Martin's *post hoc* reasoning still seems, even after a decade and a half, almost bizarrely unfounded, as if it had been written by some local tourist board. What seems mildly ironic about Martin's book is that he often doesn't sound like a Californian at all; but then one notices that his Ph.D is English and that his text, for unknown reasons, was printed in Hong Kong — and for either or both reasons, follows British practices. Martin seems almost haughty when he quibbles with Steinbeck's dialogue in *Sweet Thursday:*

> Like Harte and Twain after the Gold Rush, Steinbeck had turned his back on his homeland, loudly declaring its provincialism, treachery and unsophistication. Now, however, he had the temerity to exploit the old picturesque types that had brought his early successes. Whereas in those successes the tendency to make stage-Californians instead of living characters had been tempered by everyday experience, here the tendency goes unchecked. The result is both arrogant and inaccurate.
>
> . . . Steinbeck, whose ear for dialect had once been a source of pride, fails in *Sweet Thursday* for the first time, and fails distressingly. (101)

My goodness, the high cost of moving!

In the same year, Ungar released Joseph R. Millichap's *Steinbeck and Film*. Millichap is doggedly concerned with the writer's connection with the medium, rather than with novelistic values themselves. Thus, French and Morsberger are lucky to have been mentioned at all, even in a concluding bibliography. Yet Millichap clearly knows his subject, though he accepts as givens the standard judgments about Steinbeck's career; his own scholarship is impeccable.

In fact, Millichap is the sort of film aficionado who can seamlessly weave together criticism and plot summary. In the latter case, his efforts mirror a time when cable television and home videotapes were not yet available; Millichap rightly assumes that many of his readers would have had no chance to actually attend screenings of some of these productions.

One was particularly controversial in its day (and still is), since in the end the work done on Steinbeck's scenario by scriptwriters MacKinlay Kantor and Jo Swerling and director Alfred Hitchcock led Steinbeck to request that his name be taken out of the credits for *Lifeboat*:

... With each rewriting Steinbeck's story was changed: Kantor heightened the allegory; Swerling provided Hollywood gloss; and Hitchcock created a thriller.

The problems are evident from the opening shot in which the credits are projected over the image of a freighter's smokestack sinking into troubled waters. The sea is rather obviously a studio tank, and the tank provides the setting of the entire film. Although the technical effects ... are very good, they never create the sense of documentary realism necessary to balance the central allegory. Instead the *ersatz* ocean visually replicates the literary cliché of desperate people thrown together by fate in a lifeboat that becomes a sort of seagoing *Stagecoach* (1939) or *Grand Hotel* (1932).

The personalities of the characters prove even more bewildering than their suspiciously impeccable Hollywood grooming after weeks at sea. Steinbeck had created types, but not stereotypes.... (Millichap 79)

This seems eminently fair and balanced, and also consistent with the prevailing opinion of the film among Steinbeckians — and Steinbeck himself.

And in fact his conclusion seems to reflect very clearly the era of his study's publication:

No American writer has better exposed the dark underside of the American Dream nor better traced the lineaments of the American Nightmare — and few have so successfully celebrated the great hope which underlies the belief in human potential. Steinbeck's best fictions always picture a paradise lost, but they posit a future paradise to be regained. The light and shadows of the best films based on them replicate the complex emotions inherent in his words. Surely an artist has no more commission than the exposure of our dark dreams and the celebration of our bright potential. (178)

What is most delicious about this approach from "outside," as it were, is Millichap's conclusive reliance on appropriately visual imagery. Note his terminology: "dark," "light," "shadows," "bright." He sounds like a period director, Fellini or Bergman perhaps, discussing his own work, and as if color photography were irrelevant. To read Steinbeck, then, *as* in effect film is by no means a bad idea; and perhaps we need more such ventures in this field, though not necessarily ones tied to specific film projects.

Two massively important projects appeared in the field in 1984. Jackson J. Benson's long-awaited full-length biography — its title reverentially gleaned from Steinbeck's own canon and his reading —

The True Adventures of John Steinbeck, Writer, emerged at last. Benson's felicitous choice of a name to put on the product of more than a decade of labor manages to make its mark on many scholarly levels at once. It plays off on the titles and subject matters of several Steinbeck works, as well as on his passionate interest in things Arthurian; it works with his final writing project, never completed, on the Arthurian tales updated; and it brings to attention the notion of Steinbeck as a Knight of the Round Table, a subject not yet seriously dealt with.

Benson had so many last-minute difficulties with the Steinbeck estate (not a matter for discussion here) that in his final revisions, he managed under the pressures of the moment to leave out the fact of Steinbeck's birth and its date! But that is all beside the point — that this richly illustrated volume of well over a thousand pages is as readable as a text by its author-subject. To those familiar with the contagiousness of such styles as the Faulknerian, this is good news indeed.

Benson is, in fact, himself a Californian and knows the Steinbeck turf intimately. While it is true that this is not in the traditional sense a "life and works" biography, Benson's knowledge of where Steinbeck himself was coming from makes for a clean and clear understanding of the earlier works without prejudice towards the later ones. One senses here a living, breathing writer in formation during the early chapters, as is not usually the case in Joseph Blotner's massive William Faulkner biography, which managed to tell all and also very little in two fat volumes. But of course, Faulkner was secretive except when it suited his interests not to be so; Steinbeck was customarily forthcoming and candid about his life and work. As a result, Steinbeck's documentation is endlessly fascinating and rewarding to the reader, while the "major American novelist of the twentieth century" seems to be capable of little more than producing boring inquiries about the status of his manuscripts and what he would be paid for them. Even Hemingway's autobiography-in-letters is a better tonic than Faulkner's; Steinbeck's is fresh air.

Many biographies attempt too much and try to tell the reader how the work emerged and what to think about it. Benson, on the other hand, gives the reader enough information about the formative process of each Steinbeck title to allow for independent and creative theorizing. For example, in a passage that ties in with the motivation for writing *Burning Bright* in 1950 and the subsequent *East of Eden*, Benson succinctly puts forth the motivation probably in Steinbeck's mind without forcing the issue:

> In *East of Eden* Steinbeck adds a further element, prompted by his own recent struggle to survive and his concern for the future of his sons: in this materialistic, mechanistic universe, is there any chance for the individual to affect his own destiny? (For despite his using a biblical metaphor, the nature of the universe as he saw it had not changed.) His answer was a guarded "yes" — yes, to some extent under some circumstances. It remains a question still of whether man can see things as they are or not; if he can, he then has some freedom to act or at least to *be* different from what might be predicted on the basis only of genes and environment. (Benson, *Adventures* 668)

Having said this much, Benson hands the means to expanded insight over to the critical reader, returning to his own primarily biographical concerns:

> In other words, his boys might survive being raised by the mother who also gave them part of their blood heritage. They *need* not follow in *anyone's* footsteps. Once they see, they can choose, and to help them see, he would present in detail another heritage, another set of genes, that to him seemed more blessed and even creatively heroic, that was also theirs. In giving his book to them, he was, in effect, leaving his last will and testament and, for whatever good it might do them, his blessing. In the back of his mind he feared that like his parents he would die relatively young; he felt very strongly that this novel might very well be the last major effort he would be able to make. (668)

Steinbeck lived on more than sixteen years longer; but this indisputably true pair of paragraphs is probably the fairest and most lucid analysis of the connections between Steinbeck's life and the entangled double plots of *East of Eden*.

But this is typical of Benson's methods and success. Yet in the end he hands his materials over to the reader for resolution; the final section, entitled "The Last Battle," concerns not only Steinbeck's Vietnam days, his last stint as a war correspondent in 1967, but also the subsequent change in his opinions about the war that curiously paralleled the sudden decline in his own health. Steinbeck's last days are described in appropriately moving detail but wholly unmawkishly (1036–38). The funeral details are recited briefly and objectively, and then the book is over and conclusions about its subject, as about his novels, are left to us.

There have been other attempts at a biography of John Steinbeck of various qualities; Benson's is indispensable.

Just as indispensable in its own right is Robert DeMott's *Steinbeck's Reading: A Catalogue of Books Owned and Borrowed,* the other "big" book of 1984. As Astro hoped at the time of their publication, Benson's and DeMott's texts are not in competition with one another, since the subject of Steinbeck's reading receives little emphasis from Benson; instead, the two volumes are truly complementary, and scholars and critics have been happily ransacking both of them for fifteen years now.

Steinbeck was an inveterate reader from his younger days, and his earliest writings show the influences of a number of writers, particularly those popular at the time (if often forgotten today), many of whom swept the novice author along in their wakes for a time while he sought his own distinctive voice.

Part of what came to be seen and planned as DeMott's "Steinbeck trilogy," *Steinbeck's Reading* is the first of a trio of quite different studies (eventually issued by three different publishers), as will be seen later on. DeMott, a professor at Ohio University who at that time was the Director of the Steinbeck Research Center, provides a meticulously assembled and annotated list of titles Steinbeck was at some time known to have owned (in some cases, of course, it is not possible to prove he actually read them all) often annotated not only as to specific editions (when known) but through exhaustive scholarship producing key references throughout Steinbeck's writings.

For Steinbeck's work is unusually, almost uniquely rife with references to the books by other people — something that applies to the fiction as well as to the essays, letters, and journalism. In short, Steinbeck was a writer unashamed to be taken for a reader, and his narrators often do not see it necessary to be taken for someone without a bookshelf; his beloved Malory was only the start of his list of allusions. Indeed, DeMott lists nearly a thousand separate titles in the main portion of his volume, and he follows it with more detailed notes about his books' provenances. Not surprisingly, the text is outfitted with a full index and fascinating illustrations.

Moreover, there is even unusually detailed annotation for DeMott's solid introduction, whose splendid concluding paragraph is worth quoting in full:

> Clearly, books occupied a momentous position in Steinbeck's life and art. The poetics of reading — whether for inspiration, creative atmosphere, general background, specific information, pure pleasure, or a host of other less well defined reasons — significantly shaped Steinbeck's sense of artistic place, as well as his creative and personal

identity. "Home," he announced to Carlton Sheffield in 1964, is "only that place where the books are kept.". . . In the enormous implications of that statement, Steinbeck fulfilled a condition he had been working towards all of his life. It was nothing less than a way of living and acting in the world. (DeMott, *Reading* lv)

Steinbeck's definition of "home" is thus a ruggedly intellectual and independent-minded one, at odds with the more famous pathos (or bathos) of Frost's "where . . . they have to take you in." There is no hint of weakness in John Steinbeck's notion of home, which he might easily have hardened by having had recourse to the frequent distinction between it and "house" (implying warehouse, or storage space). The divorce that cost him books thus constituted the cruelest alimony of all.

DeMott's introduction is particularly rich as regards Steinbeck's later years, when he covers Steinbeck's final binge of research into the particularities and actualities of Malory's *Morte*. It seems clear enough that Steinbeck identified with Lancelot, a flawed enough human being with whom Malory (and through him, Steinbeck) merged. Thus once again Steinbeck's biography — in this case, his reading — and his art tally, since the practice of inserting the authorial self by one means or another became standard during the final decades of Steinbeck's career. DeMott's work makes it possible to argue along these lines because of his presentation of the evidence of Steinbeck's reading.

As an interesting aside, DeMott is the unique expert on Steinbeck's use of a volume he grew up with, *Dr. Gunn's Family Medicine* (xxxix-xlii). DeMott draws upon this volume and his knowledge of it to underscore the fictionist's delineation of pathologies, particularly of Kate (Trask) in *East of Eden*.

DeMott fundamentally recognizes that "[f]or Steinbeck, reading and writing constituted the 'creative life': at their best, as a unified field of endeavor, both were compelling acts; furthermore, in the latter stages of his career, they became redemptive processes as well" (xix). Robert DeMott's career has fairly consistently focused on the process by which Steinbeck's knowledge of what had gone before became — by a process of recycling, if you will — new art, unashamed of its parentage and almost for that reason, redemptive.

In 1985 again only two new titles emerged, one major and one distinctly minor (if only because of length, scope, and series-title inhibitions). Louis Owens's *John Steinbeck's Re-Vision of America* deals with what are usually considered the major Steinbeck fictions, and it does so in a refreshingly non-chronological manner. He emphasizes the works set in California, not so much out of the tired regional biases noted above, but because the idea of "California" has for him (and, he suggests, John Steinbeck) assumed the mythic function as the place American dreams aspire to, and then very often die.

Owens seizes upon a ledger note written by Steinbeck as early as 1929 in which Owens quotes Steinbeck as saying, "The new eye is being opened here in the west — the new seeing. It is probable no one will know it for two hundred years'." Owens goes on from this happy discovery to set forth the parameters of his study:

> Steinbeck's California fiction — all of his finest work — represents a lifelong attempt to open this "new eye," to awaken America to the failure at the heart of the American Dream and provide an alternative to that dream. The "new seeing" Steinbeck proposed would exchange the myth of an American Eden, with its dangerous flaws, for the ideal of commitment — commitment to what Steinbeck called "the one inseparable unit man plus his environment." (Owens, *Re-Vision* 3)

Owens finishes his opening by noting that "In nearly every story or novel he wrote, Steinbeck strove to hold the failed myth up to the light of everyday reality and to stress the necessity of commitment to place and to man as a way out of the wasteland defined by writers of the twenties" (3–4).

Owens's chapter organization, then, represents a healthy departure from the usual approach to Steinbeck's canon, and certainly from the heretofore standard (and increasingly obsolete) series formats of the first two decades of Steinbeck criticism. He groups works together under the rubrics "The Mountains," "The Valleys," "The Sea" (the latter does not deal at all with the nonfiction, and perhaps had been better entitled "The Shore," as Owens admits (160) — though *The Log from the Sea of Cortez* gets its fair share of mention throughout) with a final chapter on "*The Winter of Our Discontent* and the American Conscience."

In his "Sea" chapter, Owens prefaces his treatment of the Doc (Ed Ricketts) figure in *In Dubious Battle, Cannery Row,* and *Sweet Thursday* by appropriately considering the first notable appearance of such a figure, Dr. Phillips in the bizarrely unforgettable short story "The Snake":

> "The Snake" is important in itself as one of Steinbeck's finest stories, a well-crafted window between the known and unknown, conscious and unconscious realities, between the objective world of the laboratory and the subject world below and surrounding it. It is also important because of the insight it provides into the Ricketts character so central to the novels. The aloneness of Dr. Phillips reappears as the tragic alienation of Doc Burton in Steinbeck's strike novel and devel-

ops into the detachment and loneliness of Doc in *Cannery Row*. It re-appears in a diluted and sentimentalized form in *Sweet Thursday*. (164)

Though by now attention has shifted somewhat to figures in his works that seem based on Steinbeck himself, Owens's succinct summation is generally accepted.

Given the implied direction of his arrangement of materials, it is not surprising that Owens joins the increasing number of newer critics who find *East of Eden* worth more serious attention than it had received to date. Owens's handling of the Adamic theme comes to a natural apogee, therefore, when he considers *Eden's* Trask brothers:

> Adam Trask is the most unmistakable Adam in American literature, an Adam who destroys or damages his own life and the lives of others through his blind refusal to see evil. Together, Adam and his brother Charles represent what Clifford Laurence Lewis has termed the "split in American consciousness," that dialogue between good and evil which began with the first colonists. Adam symbolizes the American obsession with the idea of America as a new, unfallen world and embodies that train of thought and emotion that gave birth to the image R. W. B. Lewis has called "the American Adam." Charles, on the other hand, represents the dark side of the American consciousness, the Puritan certainty of evil as a palpable absolute. . . . Both brothers stand for absolutes, and it is this element in the American consciousness — the illusion of absolute good and evil — that Steinbeck is isolating and condemning through these two characters. (145–46)

In effect, Benson and Owens complement one another on this Adamic aspect of *Eden*, Benson achieving his insights from a biographical perspective and Owens a thematic one buttressed by theory.

Not surprisingly, then, Owens ends his study by considering *Winter*, a novel that argues for the necessity of each person's being able to live as a combination of both good and evil tendencies; in the process, Owens convincingly argues, Steinbeck has finally fully ratified the importance of the individual conscience:

> In *The Winter of Our Discontent*, for the first time, Steinbeck shifts his focus squarely onto the individual and illuminates the enormous and lonely responsibility each individual bears for his own moral existence. It is here that Ethan as character achieves much greater impact than any previous Steinbeck character, surpassing in the power of his tragic implications such successful archetypes and symbols as Joseph Wayne, Jim Nolan, Lennie and George, Ma and Tom Joad. For, as Ethan

says, in a statement that flirts with sentimentality, "It's so much darker when a light goes out than it would have been if it had never shone." (207)

Owens ultimately concludes that it is Steinbeck's tracking of this distinctly American moral dilemma that marks him as of permanent worth. For

> Like his heroes, Steinbeck was committed to a quest for understanding, an attempt to open the "new eye" in the West and throughout America. As his last poignant adventure with Charley suggests, Steinbeck's life was spent "In Search of America." (209)

Rather than flirting with "sentimentality," then, Ethan's reflections upon starlight can be seen as his own answer to his stated wish never to have been born. The unborn can do no harm, but neither can they do good. A star that has never "shone" may be unmissed in a sense, but in another, its "light" is quite useless.

But this is not to put words into the mouth of the author of an important study of the American ethos as seen through the writings of John Steinbeck.

The other 1985 title was a volume of mine entitled *John Steinbeck: Life, Work, and Criticism* and published by a small press series out of Fredericton, New Brunswick, York Press, which imposed serious series discipline on its titles. The result is a monograph which, whether or not still available, is of primary use to high-schoolers of a higher level of capability and, certainly, university undergraduates in their first two years of study. This series-format number is highly topicalized and compartmentalized, if sound and, necessarily, dated in some respects. In fairness to myself, I should note that the publisher allotted neither space nor encouragement for more than summaries of prior work and received information.

In the following year, two studies emerged, both of great value. Mimi Reisel Gladstein published *The Indestructible Woman in Faulkner, Hemingway, and Steinbeck* (1986). This is of course a study of three authors, and the material it covers reflects the author's observation that since the book's inception as a dissertation project in 1973, "close to 2000 items on Faulkner, approximately 1500 on Hemingway, and about 350 on Steinbeck" had been listed in MLA indices (Gladstein, xi). Gladstein's book in fact reflects that proportion, but she is more "concerned that this work might somehow be interpreted as demonstrating that Faulkner, Hemingway, and Steinbeck were nascent feminists because of their depictions of such strong and indomitable women" (xi). Again, and not to attempt to speak for Gladstein, it would seem that these writers, all involved in their own lives with strikingly strong females, were simply baffled by the women they had been attracted to even though "they all three exhibited chauvinistic and sexist traits. If anything, the indestructible woman is a projection of that sexism" (xi). Gladstein goes on to excuse the three authors from any "condemnation" since as "children of their times," they did not have the "benefit" of the experience of "consciousness-raising in the sixties" (xii). (Indeed, they had had enough of the sixties, all three of them, to expire in them.) Can a critic who uses the term "chauvinistic" as though it had a single application avoid condescending when discussing the works of these "children of their times"?

Yet, thankfully. Gladstein notes the proximity of the death dates of those "children" (102) and notes that these writers' "indestructible women are a re-creation of the bountiful and nurturing mother" who, in childhood, is "the mother we all want when we are sick or hurt. Rare is the individual who doesn't long for the irresponsibility of childhood when mother was there to fix it all or make it better" (110). Gladstein would probably quickly admit that all of us, critics included, are "children of their times," and that there is something of the enlightened 1960s in her own sound conclusion:

> For the men with dependent and self-destructive personalities, longing for a simpler world, woman personifies what he is not, the *other*. The dependent man, then, would project a dependable other; the self-destructive man, and indestructible other. For men who all had terrible bouts with depression, is it not appropriate that the *other* should also serve as a symbol of optimism? (111)

Gladstein displays apt middle-period feminist critical technique here; she goes beyond earlier readings of Steinbeck's female characters, yet is mercifully free of the theoretical and prejudicial readings of the 1990s. As an almost random selection from her insights, one might adduce her commentary on the Lopez sisters in *The Pastures of Heaven*, who become whores without giving the deed its name, and who at least superficially seem comically drawn:

> . . . What Steinbeck seems to be saying is that the two women have the strength to deceive themselves when they can, thus making their prostitution more palatable, but they also face up to harsh reality when they must. Men, in Steinbeck's stories, often collapse when they have to discard their illusions. Adaptability is one of the characteristics that most of his indestructible women, like the Lopez sisters, share. In

that way Steinbeck's characterization implies a Darwinian precedent, in keeping with his biological view of humanity. (91)

One may be reminded here of the women at Harry Hope's in Eugene O'Neill's *The Iceman Cometh*, Margie, Cora, and Pearl — all three names making the same ironic implications of purity — who refuse to be called "whores" but who will allow themselves to be called "tarts."

Gladstein makes her central point clearest, including what the naive reader might not at first appreciate, as she approaches her final page:

> . . . But for Faulkner, Hemingway, and Steinbeck it is as often as not the dehumanized or sketchily drawn woman whose indestructibility is celebrated. The scarcity of fully drawn women in Hemingway and Steinbeck results from their male focus, their absorption with the male quest. (110)

Although I am not covering mere chapters about Steinbeck here, I have included Gladstein because Mimi Gladstein has included what is essentially substantial separate material about Steinbeck folded into the matrix of a carefully unified study of three major writers and their often parallel characteristics.

Gladstein's own critical perspective was at an early stage here, paying a degree of homage to previous writers; yet she is also fair in noting, non-judgmentally, that Steinbeck does not as a rule depart from the old observed concept of women as possessed of received, instinctual wisdom, and men as the prisoners of their own intellectual obsessions. (And she also casually tosses in a grace note about Darwinism, something to which Brian Railsback, as we shall see later on, devotes an entire volume.) Her book is thus best seen as a safely walked bridge to things to come.

The year's second (and major) title brought a new voice to the fore: that of John H. Timmerman, professor at Calvin College in Grand Rapids. *John Steinbeck's Fiction: The Aesthetics of the Road Taken* discusses Steinbeck's artistic choices and the patterns throughout his career that those choices illuminate. Timmerman begins with an essay on "Steinbeck as Literary Artist," in which he sets forth a fresh division of Steinbeck's artistic concerns in a way that defuses much prior single-focus discussion, whether positive or negative:

> With the exception of his clear and forthright Nobel Prize Address, which Steinbeck claimed to have rewritten at least twenty times, one must rely on extrapolation from letters and random statements in fictional works to reconstruct Steinbeck's artistic beliefs. While each of these will be developed further in analysis of major works, three es-

sential artistic premises that govern the making of the work warrant
attention here: storytelling, realism, and "hooptedoodle." (Timmerman, *Aesthetics* 4–5)

Timmerman's deliberate choice of a quote from a familiar Frost poem
does not disguise the problem it presents us with, one apparent after a
first reading of the Frost piece as well: the inseparability of conscious
and instinctive decisions, even aesthetic ones, in the creation of a work
of art; and the resultant necessity of living with such commitments once
made — or of finding ways around the commitment.

Timmerman is right to sense in Steinbeck's writing this triple tradition: storytelling as practiced in the West for millennia, the dominant
realism of the present century, and the more experimental and free-
wheeling "hooptedoodle," to which Steinbeck alludes in *Sweet Thursday* — a fun piece for the most part, but with some darker implications.
Timmerman observes:

> In some instances, however, hooptedoodle is simply indulgence of
> the author's fancy and has virtually nothing to do with the plot. . . .
> (13)

Although Timmerman spots a valid third trait in Steinbeck's fiction, he
does not give it full credit for its role in a leading movement of his —
Timmerman's — time: the reflexive or self-referential experimental fiction of the 1970s and 1980s that included such practitioners as Kurt
Vonnegut, Donald Barthelme, John Barth, Thomas Pynchon, Richard
Brautigan, and several others. Timmerman is wise enough to recognize
a method in Steinbeck's seeming "indulgence."

Timmerman is perhaps the only critic, except for Robert DeMott,
who has looked at all three paisano and Cannery Row novels on their
own terms, without trying to impose external critical referents on them.
Thus he and DeMott have been among the few with a kind word to say
about *Sweet Thursday*. He does so by setting the book in the ancient
tradition of farce:

> . . . The cliché one wants to avoid is "good-natured" farce, but that is
> part of its definition; farce is good-natured in that it recognizes the
> limitations, foibles, and capacity for wrong in human nature but also
> the essential good.
>
> Consider first how the tone of farce is established in the novel,
> and second how the story exhibits certain specific traits of farce. Suc-
> cessful farce depends on a light and detached authorial tone, which
> Steinbeck establishes in several ways. The author is present in the
> work, in a narrative tone that is faintly admonishing but never angry,

like a realistic but loving and unpatronizing grandfather watching his slightly removed progeny from a distance. One observes this in the descriptions of setting. Cannery Row is in the afterglow of its heyday; the factories are largely silent, life has settled into a postwar slowness. This is an occasion not for a sense of loss but for fond realism . . . (172)

Timmerman's genial reading, open-minded and fresh, seems to rescue this late work from a history of critical crabbiness. He also notices how "Steinbeck humanizes and locates the comedy of *Sweet Thursday* — in religion. A dominant motif in *Tortilla Flat* and a darkened absence in *Cannery Row*, religion resurfaces in *Sweet Thursday* in a farcical and human fashion" (175).

Exactly how Steinbeck brings this off is left to the curious reader to recognize, but it is clear that Timmerman is a new kind of Steinbeck critic, one with no interest in imposing his strictures on an artist errant. Timmerman judges Steinbeck's work in terms of "three elements," "his genius for character, story, and language" that are "Steinbeck's greatest strength and, when they fall short, his greatest weakness" (273). In sum, Timmerman's topically sectioned volume remains of enduring value because he recognized the "roads" Steinbeck took although he was often in sympathetic disagreement with the choices the writer made.

Next, R. S. Hughes's *Beyond the Red Pony: A Reader's Companion to Steinbeck's Complete Short Stories* (1987) was a first of its kind. Though in terms of its standard Scarecrow structure it seems meant for school use, that is, for high school student and undergraduates, it is also the first meticulous story-by-story journey through Steinbeck's writing for the shorter form, dealing not only with the (then) "uncollected" pieces of the 1940s and 1950s, but also with the novice writing Steinbeck concocted as an occasional Stanford student in the 1920s. In his coverage of the latter Hughes includes considerable scholarship in the interest of establishing provenance.

Hughes is so thorough that he gives attention to the "intercalary" chapters, or interchapters, in *The Grapes of Wrath, Cannery Row*, and *Sweet Thursday*, as though they were actually separable short stories — which, it can be argued, the ones in the second and third novels are. Indeed, the presence of these chapters is frequently used to arm charges that one or both books are structurally defective. Hughes, as usual not wanting to venture very far into new critical approaches, concludes in his section on *Sweet Thursday*:

Both of these *Sweet Thursday* interchapters are ironic and mildly humorous; yet neither furthers the main plot concerning the romance of Doc and Suzy. Though we might grant that these two interchapters add a certain tone or atmosphere, both are essentially isolated from the rest of the novel in terms of plot and character. They also indicate a gradual shift in the subject matter of Steinbeck's short fiction from serious domestic issues . . . to the humorous. . . . (Hughes, *Beyond* 118)

That shift is palpable, yet one can argue for the validity of the inclusion of these interchapters in different terms rather than as instances of Steinbeck cleaning out his files and stuffing his new manuscripts, even for purposes of humor. Beyond "tone or atmosphere" alone — assuming a deliberate authorial strategy on Steinbeck's part — such chapters serve as a means of delaying "plot and character" development, of downplaying the centrality of the plot about Doc and Suzy in favor of, perhaps, the sense of place and of time. Steinbeck may also be claiming his right as author to intrude upon his own narrative in (perhaps) a postmodern (or premodern) way — as though authorial self-effacement were not in truth a ruse as well.

Hughes's book is briefly, or perhaps more properly, modestly concluded. He recognizes Steinbeck's special genius at the short story form and acknowledges that he has brought attention to the fact that Steinbeck wrote at least twice as many stories as he was usually given credit for. One can only wonder what Steinbeck's career output might have been if he had been born five years earlier and/or responded to the heady magazine market circumstances of the thirties even sooner, but already in full possession of his talents.

There now follow in quick succession two anthologies of criticism put forth under the name of the distinguished critic Harold Bloom, who seems to feel licensed to speak out on all writers everywhere and of whatever era. The patronizing tone in evidence here did not endear him to an audience of Steinbeck aficionados at one Steinbeck conference (to which he seemed to have thought he had descended, or condescended, as from clouds). In the earlier volume, *John Steinbeck* (in the Chelsea House Modern Critical Views series), Bloom has assembled a good if naturally quite arbitrary anthology of previously published materials — eleven pieces in all, including a three-page anecdote by the late Anthony Burgess, a surprising presence but a reliably entertaining and erudite one. Yet a good many of these pieces originally appeared in books already considered here, some so recently that reprinting was probably premature.

The following year, the same publisher issued (in its Modern Critical Interpretations series) another Bloom anthology of criticism, *John Steinbeck's "The Grapes of Wrath."* This time there are only eight entries, but some of them reduplicate inclusions in the previous volume. We are naturally puzzled as to why. Only a single essay, Frederick I. Carpenter's ubiquitous 1941 "The Philosophical Joads," represents a look back to the earliest days of Steinbeck criticism; and thus one might wonder wherein the value of these paired assemblages lies, excellently turned out as they are.

That leaves us pondering the presence of Bloom himself, unfortunately confined largely to an introduction of just over four pages and repeated from book to book. Moreover, about half of that space is given over to long block quotations from Emerson, Hemingway, and Steinbeck — a strategy many a harried scholar-critic will recognize as a great saver of time, not to mention work and thought. Bloom seems unable to progress from the antiquely narrow conceptions of Steinbeck as Emersonian (Carpenter's, 1941) or as a writer deliberately embracing a quasi-biblical mode of expression (as if that were the *only* point to Steinbeck's descriptive techniques). Bloom has been at the forefront of preserving traditional critical values in the face of postmodernist and later theories; but name the right names though he will, he does not allay the suspicion that his reading of Steinbeck — and Steinbeck criticism — is for the most part nearly half a century out of touch.

Let the reader judge the tone of Bloom's introduction's conclusion:

> I remain uneasy about my own experience of rereading *The Grapes of Wrath*. Steinbeck is not one of the inescapable American novelists of our century; he cannot be judged in close relation to Cather, Dreiser, and Faulkner, Hemingway and Fitzgerald, Nathanael West, Ralph Ellison, and Thomas Pynchon. Yet there are no canonical standards worthy of human respect that could exclude *The Grapes of Wrath* from a serious reader's esteem. Compassionate narrative that addresses itself so directly to the great social questions of its era is simply too substantial a human achievement to be dismissed. Whether a human strength, however generously worked through, is also an aesthetic value, in a literary narrative, is one of those larger issues that literary criticism scarcely knows how to decide. One might desire *The Grapes of Wrath* to be composed differently, whether as [to] plot or as [to] characterization, but wisdom compels one to be grateful for the novel's continued existence. (Bloom 1987, 5; Bloom 1988, 5)

Surely there is a "to" missing in Bloom's last sentence, but that is not to the point. Just as surely we are all relieved not to have to deal with all of the rest of what Steinbeck wrote. One wonders about the future fate of Pynchon's reputation, even without challenging it. The frequently turgid Dreiser? The wonderful and unknown Nathanael West, whose existence has to be averred to many a student by many a professor?

Bloom's comparative examples, then, seem a bit on the bizarre side; but in fairness to him, he does in both books include an editor's note thanking the editorial assistants — one per volume — who, one infers, did the field research for each volume. But this sort of acknowledgment is generally included in an essay called just that, whereas in these books the term refers to sources and permissions. One longs here for the sort of incisive and thorough presentation of included texts that are routine for, say, Warren French — and many another Steinbeck scholar. Then, too, Bloom invites irony, and if he wants to be patronizing with respect to being "grateful for the novel's continued existence" he is welcome to be so; but if Steinbeck is "not one of the inescapable American novelists of our century," Steinbeck's readership has news for him: He can run but he can't hide.

The American Festival Theatre brought the first authorized stage production of *Grapes* to Edinburgh in 1987. The following year, adaptor Peter Whitebrook (with Duncan Low) published *Staging Steinbeck: Dramatising "The Grapes of Wrath"* in London. This is not a text, but an illustrated journal of the steps leading to the production and the problems encountered along the way. Just as any stage production constitutes an interpretation, adaptations constitute criticism. Admittedly, this is specialized matter, but it is included here for at least part of our readership; it is a fascinating and full account.

Thomas Fensch, whose primary field is journalism, issued a most useful edition of Steinbeck's interviews in the same year, *Conversations with John Steinbeck*. Because these short pieces involve the interplay of Steinbeck's mind with a variety — some twenty-six — of interviewers representing a number of approaches and perspectives, the book creates an image of Steinbeck's emerging sense of a public self (guarded, playful, whatever), the anthology can be called a miniature intellectual autobiography. The full uses of this collection have hardly been tapped to date. Fensch's editing and commentary are minimal.

That is to observe that Fensch surveys the field of Steinbeck interviews in his introduction, noting along the way how Steinbeck's changing attitudes reflect a changing world about him. Though Steinbeck's Vietnam reportage is both controversial and not allowed to be reprinted as yet, Fensch summarizes Steinbeck's attitude towards what he called "Vietnicks" — young people opposed to the war while also safely at home:

> This view, which brought Steinbeck's friends so much agony, is seldom brought up in interviews, and they just do not reflect the extent of his involvement with the Vietnam war. Perhaps reporters did not know of the anguish he caused his friends or did not think it diplomatic to broach the subject of Vietnam in an interview during those trying years. After he won the Nobel Prize, reporters may have felt even more reluctant to press him strongly on the war. The subject was a key Steinbeck dilemma during his final years, just as it was the watershed issue during the administration of Lyndon Johnson. (Fensch xv)

Thus Fensch posits for his readers materials not present in his actual anthology, which is also in effect a substantial addition to the (republished) Steinbeck canon.

Thereafter, Fensch brings his own interview survey to concentrated form in a very few but accurate sentences:

> Throughout his life, Steinbeck, as interview subject, remained remarkably straightforward; he shied away from details of his life, but did eventually answer most questions about himself. He did not wish to have his picture taken (and only much later did his picture appear on any of the dust jackets of his books). And he did not recreate his persona in fictional form. Nor did he weave half-truths about his life or create myths about himself. Ultimately, Steinbeck kept his own values, his own compass throughout his life: he insisted on his privacy, he did not become a public lecturer, and he chose to experiment in form and style from book to book. (Fensch xv)

All true — if the line about recreating the persona in fictional form refers only to interviews, as suggested initially, and not to Steinbeck's fiction itself.

Jackson J. Benson published the volume of interest of 1988, though a maverick one. His fifteen-year quest of the Steinbeck grail, which he describes as the author's "ghost" (*Looking for Steinbeck's Ghost*), is more than the study sweepings from the period of his ordeal. Profusely illustrated, it is also the record of an astonishingly difficult pursuit of persons often very hard to trace and, for valid reasons of their own, reclusive in character. Seldom enough do we find biographies worthy of notice because of their subjects, or the quality of their biographers' labors, to demand a sequel. And how often on both grounds?

Benson encountered grief galore in his career shift from Hemingway (not an abandonment), via Malamud, to John Steinbeck; and thus he and perhaps Mimi Gladstein are the figures (pace Harold Bloom) who ought to be compared. Gladstein had a critical cause to pursue, Benson had paid his dues, and Bloom was like an alien making a brief visit to earth. For Benson was, like Gladstein, a late starter, and his prologue endears the reader to the man at once, telling of how he encountered his own version of the "publish or perish" mentality in the form of serious advice from an academic adviser, after which Benson "wrote a book on Hemingway . . . and also published a couple of articles":

> These, then, were the impressive credentials that I brought with me to New York and to Mrs. John Steinbeck for the most important interview, or series of interviews, of my life. If you were the widow of one of the most famous writers of our time, would you pick this man to do his biography? (Benson, *Looking* 19)

Of course, this is a book about the writing of a book, and in a sense contains much that the original biography could not. In that way it is specialist material of primary interest to someone already familiar with the biography's attainments. But on the one hand, it is hardly without a set of valid critical observations of its own; and on the other, it is hard not to imagine even a reader scarcely sure of who John Steinbeck was — like the tourists flooding today's Cannery Row — enjoying it for its own sake, as a kind of literary detective work, something by Raymond Chandler, perhaps.

Consider, if you will, the tongue-in-cheek comic menace implied by Benson's chapter titles: "In the Big City," "Lost in High Tech," "The Search for the Early Life," "High Anxiety," "Biographer as Detective," "Gwyn and Kate: Two Women in His Life," "Coping with the Famous," "Fear, Envy, and Loathing," "Looking for Steinbeck's Ghost," "The Joys of Being Threatened," and "Pride and Prejudice." Benson's self-portrayal as kind of literary Inspector Clouseau is endearing, and it would take a mean spirit to want to "give away the ending" to a detective work, even a nonfictional one. Suffice it to say that much of this matter had been printed before, and that Benson's Hemingway/Hunter Steinbeck/Farmer essay forms much of this book's conclusion.

Benson's own humaneness, especially after what a decade of work on Steinbeck had put him through, is apparent when he considers the effects of the attacks on Steinbeck from the Left and Right over the years, and particularly the "nastiness" of mindless vitriol hurled by such critics as Mary McCarthy and Stanley Edgar Hyman:

> The sad part of the pattern of violent political attack that followed the novelist was that it was a red herring. It detracted from the fact

that he had a number of important things to say. As early as the mid-1930s he was talking about man living in harmony with nature, condemning a false sense of progress, advocating love and acceptance, condemning the nearly inevitable use of violence, and preaching ecology at a time when not even very many scientists cared about it. When he talked about the human "species" and the need to live in harmony with the whole of nature and the need to adapt (if homo sapiens does not, some other species will, he pointed out), he might as well have been talking Martian, as far as most literary critics were concerned. (196–97)

As Benson's fascinating book (full of premonitory lore for anyone contemplating writing a biography, especially of an author only recently deceased) comes to its ending, he has come to identify with his subject but, like that subject, he has not failed in objectivity or fallen into a slough of defensive self-pity.

Benson's "ending," of course, is the biography itself. By a similar if reversed process, Louis Owens's 1989 *"The Grapes of Wrath": Trouble in the Promised Land* is a kind of sequel to his prior critical study of the Steinbeck canon. The subtitle to the subtitle is "A Student's Companion to the Novel," and though this is part of Twayne's "Masterwork Studies" series, Owens does not seem to have been constrained by any artificially imposed format directives. His chapters take on *Grapes* from a number of perspectives, so that in the end the perspectives offer a real sense of three-dimensionality. Nor does Owens talk down to his "student" readerships.

The reader who knows that Louis Owens himself has some American Indian heritage might rush headlong towards his eighth chapter, "'Grampa Killed Indians, Pa Killed Snakes': The American Indian and *The Grapes of Wrath*." (The very title is ominous.) Here Owens cheats a bit, but originally and creatively, making this an essay on "Indian" presences in all of Steinbeck rather than simply the "significant and little noted one" that animates the great novel (Owens, *Trouble* 58). Explaining his title quotation, Owens notes that the casual references to Indians in passages such as the one quoted in his title show that in *Grapes,* "the Indian is of significance only as a symbol of the destructive consciousness underlying American settlement and the westering pattern. He has mythic dimension but no further reality" (60). Therefore, Owens consults the rest of Steinbeck's works for an essay that fascinates even as it seems to violate the parameters of his assignments, but valuably. If his conclusion bothers any, he might suggest that that is because

Steinbeck, according to the day's ethos, accepted a portrait of Depression California that is startlingly devoid of minorities:

> In *The Grapes of Wrath*, a novel that on one crucial level cries out at injustice, the figure of the Indian is index and symbol but no more. In Steinbeck's great novel, as in most American literature, the Indian remains merely an abstraction, an "Injun Joe" mirror reflecting back at America its own fantasies and its own guilt. The real Indian is finally subsumed, through the vehicle of literature, into the self-consciousness of white America that is portrayed in this novel, becoming that America's shadow and ceasing to exist in its own right. That this transformation should take place within the pages of *The Grapes of Wrath* should be no surprise, for surely this is the most quintessentially American of novels. (64)

Owen's study is valuable as much for what it did but was not expected to do as for what it was commissioned to do.

In fact, Owens simply did all he was asked to do; the Indian chapter was something he must have felt he had to write, and in the process he created one of the book's most original moments. This is Owens's high praise for *Grapes* early in his study:

> In American literature only one novel had previously brought together the political, sociological, and aesthetic power found in *The Grapes of Wrath*: Mark Twain's *Adventures of Huckleberry Finn,* with its searing indictment of the South, of the institution of slavery, and of the human conscience, and its unequalled brilliance in the use of a vernacular narrator. (9)

This writer remembers strolling, on a break from a Steinbeck conference a few years ago, through the churchyard of San Juan Bautista Mission in California. While one of us was fascinated by historical architecture, Owens drew attention to the thousands of Indians buried there in a small space, worked perhaps to death by the missionaries who wanted the mission built. Different perceptions of the same locale? There are all sorts of slaveries, and Owens's study of *Grapes* is a valuable corrective.

In fact, there were not one but five fine volumes issued in 1989. As Jackson Benson said at the end of a conference keynote address at about this time, one in which he basically reprised his biographical approach throughout both his volumes, he was able to signal his audience with a jubilant, "We won," meaning that at long last the nay-sayers needed not be listened to any longer. Steinbeck studies were off and running on their own.

In that same year, R. S. Hughes brought forth a Twayne study that goes beyond his earlier Scarecrow title dealing with Steinbeck's shorter works: *John Steinbeck: A Study of the Short Fiction.* "Chip" Hughes manages to defeat any series-format constrictions this time by ending his own verbal presence about two-thirds of the way into the volume, if thereafter with reprinted matter by other hands. Thus Hughes is simultaneously able to satisfy his publisher and maintain his own critical integrity as one of perhaps only two experts on the Steinbeck short story.

Hughes recalls how "Steinbeck began telling stories early in his life. His childhood friends remember gathering in the basement of his Salinas, California, home to hear John spin yarns of ghosts and leprechauns, of 'spooks, sprites, and other invisible beings'" (Hughes, *Study* 5). Hughes's conclusion to his own introduction is markedly concise:

> Variety is the best word to describe the generic types Steinbeck employed in short fiction. He experimented with sketches, parables, beast fables, and initiation stories, and even dabbled in fairy tales and science fiction. Variety also describes his numerous themes. Whereas he championed proletarian values in his novels of the 1930s, Steinbeck focused in his short stories of that era on the problems of individual human beings. A common theme in his short fiction, as we have seen, is frustration stemming from loneliness, isolation, blocked communication, or sexual repression, and these frustrations occasionally lead to violence. In his tales of the 1930s, respectability is also a recurrent theme; and in the forties and fifties Steinbeck deals with such topical themes as divorce and nuclear holocaust. (18–19)

This is an apt summation of Steinbeck's career as a short story writer, and also a pioneering account of the differences between the prepossessions of his stories and those of his longer fictions.

Hughes's own writing resembles that of his volume for Scarecrow, and the book's second section of essays by other authors on Steinbeck and his attitudes towards story writing also contains familiar matter. Tetsumaro Hayashi complements a letter from Steinbeck (dated 1962) to his onetime writing teacher at Stanford, Edith Mirrielees, with a collection of Steinbeck's comments on the craft of story writing; this is reminiscent of a section of Hayashi's number on Steinbeck and the art of writing (Steinbeck Essay Series No. 2). The four appended essays are by Marilyn H. Mitchell, Charles E. May, M. R. Satyanarayana (a perceptive scholar from India, now deceased), and Arnold L. Goldsmith. This is a series title from Twayne that does have a clear and certain usefulness.

The year's new work includes the papers from the 1986 Steinbeck Conference at the University of Lowell, Massachusetts. *Rediscovering Steinbeck: Revisionist Views of His Art, Politics and Intellect* is the record of a lively Steinbeck meeting at a seemingly unlikely venue, a downtown Lowell recovering from the shutdown of its mills and decades of neglect. The volume's editors and the conference's hosts are Cliff Lewis, already mentioned, and Carroll Britch, a theater teacher at Springfield College. Lewis and Britch divide the printed papers into two categories: "The Artist in Process" and "The Artist in Society." These catchall titles include papers on a wide variety of subjects by such familiar figures as DeMott, Owens, Marcia Yarmus, Hughes, Gladstein (with Bobbi Gonzales), Ditsky, Tammaro, and Judith Mulcahy. I related Steinbeck to Randolph Bourne, Thom Tammaro compared him to William Least Heat-Moon, and Lewis discussed Steinbeck's connection to FDR and his speechwriting days. Others write about their recent areas of specialization, and Britch memorably performed "Breakfast" and gave a critical commentary on that story that became a part of *Grapes*. John Kenneth Galbraith was on hand to lend a certain *gravitas* to the proceedings.

This is, in short, a very mixed bag, in fact, a grab-bag of papers that go off in all directions, but energetically and therapeutically. The eventual Lewis and Britch publication is well worth the scholar's attention and it suits this chapter's rubric, but it is hard to say what other business all the papers have being together.

The Lowell conference was a great success, if not one ever to be duplicated. (Britch and Lewis have been largely silent since.) The singular feature worth noting about the editors' presentation is that each contributor gets his or her own private introduction before each essay. In the end, the Lowell conference papers are still very much worth investigating, but not for anyone who hopes to find any single major strand of new Steinbeck research showing. That may, in the end, prove a sign of health.

The year's third noteworthy volume is Robert DeMott's *John Steinbeck: Working Days, The Journals of "The Grapes of Wrath."* Steinbeck had been in the habit of writing warm-up journals to his editor, Pascal Covici, and the one written during the creation of *East of Eden* had long been in print. DeMott backtracks to the days of the writing of *Grapes*, when his first wife Carol typed up the results of each day's effort. The journals depict the writer pushing himself and full of doubts as to whether he could finish the job, which he often did while listening to classical music chosen for mood's sake and recorded on the twelve-inch

acetate discs of the era. (There exists a similar journal for the period of
the writing of *The Wayward Bus*, but as yet it has not been allowed to
see print.) There are exactly one hundred entries, and DeMott includes
subsequent entries for the post-publication 1939–1941 period. Considering the controversy aroused by the novel's celebrated ending scene, it
is of special interest to sound out the author on his last day of writing
his epic, October 26, 1938:

> Today should be a day of joy because I could finish today — just
> the walk to the barn, the new people and the ending and that's all.
> But I seem to have contracted an influenza of the stomach or some-
> thing. Anyway I am so dizzy I can hardly see the page. This makes it
> difficult to work. On the other hand, it might get worse. I might be
> in for a siege. Can't afford to take that chance. I must go on. If I can
> finish today I don't much care what happens afterwards. Wish — if it
> was inevitable, that it could have held off one more day. . . . I feel
> better — sitting here. I wish I were done. Best way is just to get down
> to the lines. I wonder if this flu could be simple and complete ex-
> haustion. I don't know. But I do know that I'll have to start at it now
> and, of course, anything I do will be that much nearer the end.
>
> Finished this day — and I hope to God it's good. (DeMott,
> *Working* 93)

The entries are carefully annotated, making it possible for the reader to
match each day's output with the specific content of the novel itself at
that point. For example, it is interesting to consider that the book's
notorious final scene, or tableau (long in the works, however) in which
a terribly sick stranger is suckled by the Joads's daughter — was apparently written by a terribly sick man sounding very much like a Beckett
protagonist. *Working Days* is so richly tapestried that it will never cease
to be a source of awe for the Steinbeckian; and of course, it is a major
addition to what we know of Steinbeck's writing, thinking, life — and
plans for his greatest novel. But given the focus of this volume, it is
DeMott's "secondary" scholarship and criticism that need to be addressed; we are not here to listen to Steinbeck's voice, but rather, to
those of his finest readers. The following is a sample of DeMott's observations about the planning of what would become the novel's four-
teenth chapter,

> . . . one of the most important theoretical chapters in the novel, and
> perhaps the most significant summation of organismal philosophy
> Steinbeck had yet written. The first half of the chapter augurs changes
> in the Western states' socioeconomic basis, and includes a paean to
> the universal human capacity for creation: "For man, unlike any other

thing organic or inorganic in the universe, grows beyond his work, walks up the stairs of his concepts, emerges ahead of his accomplishments." The second half of the chapter expresses the central core of Steinbeck's mature phalanx theory, the creation of an aggregate, dynamic "we" from distinct, myriad selves. (15)

If that doesn't drive a reader back to *Grapes* and then forward to *Working Days,* predicting reader responses has become a desperate enterprise. In short, the riches of Robert DeMott's *Working Days* have only begun to be tasted.

In March 1989, there was a Steinbeck conference in San Jose, California; and the keynote speaker was the celebrated critic of American literature Leslie Fiedler, who managed, by finishing his address with a "grace note" acknowledging the right of *Grapes* to continue to be read, to earn himself (all unknowing) the year's Harold Bloom award for graceless patronization. The conference's book sale included not only the 1988 titles but a fourth from 1989, just issued, my compilation entitled *Critical Essays on Steinbeck's "The Grapes of Wrath."* This book's title became progressively longer as its publisher seemed to feel that a prospective reader might not know whose *Grapes* was in question, but in fact, there was little series-format interference in the creation of this volume. Rather, yours truly was set loose to compile a set of largely original essays, not excluding ten original reviews which had not appeared in previous such anthologies — among which were a deathbed-permission piece by Malcolm Cowley and the vital Canadian contribution by Earle Birney. There are also some striking maps reprinted by permission of Don Morris.

Because I wanted these names in my roster, I obtained rights to an undeservedly obscure essay by Peter Lisca, and at the last minute substituted a conference paper by Warren French ("John Steinbeck and Modernism") for an autobiographical one the publisher did not cotton to. Also included at the end were essays by Christopher L. Salter on the "cultural geography" of *Grapes* and my own on the novel's ending. Otherwise, the inclusions are deliberately original and "commissioned" for no fee from the likes of Jackson J. Benson (who carpentered together two previous essays on the creation of the novel), Roy S. Simmonds (on the novel's British reception), Carroll Britch and Cliff Lewis (on the growth of the family), Louis Owens (on desentimentalizing the Joads), and Mimi Gladstein (on Ma Joad in novel and film). There is an introduction surveying fifty years of scholarship on the novel itself, and an annotated bibliography that discusses just about all prior critical writing on the novel, including of course those of article length. A decade later, this anthology does seem worth consulting.

Dividing a chapter at the arbitrary mark of the tick of the calendar makes little sense; and no one with a grasp of mathematics would take pleasure in thinking that anything miraculous took place in 1990 to mark a new decade. (For that matter, neither does 2000.) And to speak truly, the 1980s were as much a decade of vision as of revision as were the 1990s to follow. What matters in the end is that both decades show that new scholars and critics were entering the lists on various Steinbeck topics, and that older ones were giving most serious and generous attention to reconsidering their previously strongly held positions. It can be argued that the titles of these two final chapters are interchangeable: that writers such as French and Lisca had already done their first revisions, and that the works of the 1980s truly revise nothing. But to speak candidly, the decade sent Steinbeck scholarship off in a number of new directions by vanquishing old preconceptions; in that sense, it is as truly an era of revisions.

Works Consulted

Benson, Jackson J. *Looking for Steinbeck's Ghost*. Norman: U Oklahoma P, 1988.

―――. *The True Adventures of John Steinbeck, Writer*. New York: Viking Press, 1984.

Bloom, Harold, ed. *John Steinbeck*. New York: Chelsea House, 1987.

―――, ed. *John Steinbeck's "The Graces of Wrath."* New York: Chelsea House, 1988.

Davis, Robert Con, ed. *Twentieth Century Interpretations of "The Grapes of Wrath."* Englewood Cliffs, NJ: Prentice-Hall, 1982.

DeMott, Robert. *Steinbeck's Reading: A Catalogue of Books Owned and Borrowed*. New York: Garland, 1984.

―――, ed. *Working Days: The Journals of "The Grapes of Wrath."* New York: Viking Press, 1989.

Ditsky, John. *John Steinbeck: Life, Work, and Criticism*. Fredericton, NB: York P, 1985.

―――, ed. *Critical Essays on Steinbeck's "The Grapes of Wrath."* Boston: G. K. Hall, 1989.

Fensch, Thomas, ed. *Conversations with John Steinbeck*. Jackson: U P of Mississippi, 1988.

Fontenrose, Joseph. *Steinbeck's Unhappy Valley*. Berkeley, CA: Joseph Fontenrose, 1981.

Gladstein, Mimi R. *The Indestructible Woman in Faulkner, Hemingway, and Steinbeck*. Ann Arbor, MI: UMI Research Press, 1986.

Hughes, R. S. *Beyond The Red Pony: A Reader's Companion to Steinbeck's Complete Short Stories*. Metuchen, NJ: Scarecrow, 1987.

―――. *John Steinbeck: A Study of the Short Fiction*. Boston: Twayne, 1989.

Lewis, Cliff, and Carroll Britch, eds. *Rediscovering Steinbeck: Revisionist Views of His Art, Politics and Intellect*. Lewiston, NY: Edwin Mellen P, 1989.

Martin, Stoddard. *California Writers: Jack London, John Steinbeck, The Tough Guys*. New York: St. Martin's P, 1983.

Millichap, Joseph R. *Steinbeck and Film*. New York: Ungar, 1983.

Owens, Louis. *"The Grapes of Wrath": Trouble in the Promised Land*. Boston: Twayne, 1989.

―――. *John Steinbeck's Re-Vision of America*. Athens: U Georgia P, 1985.

St. Pierre, Brian. *John Steinbeck: The California Years.* San Francisco: Chronicle, 1983.

Timmerman, John H. *John Steinbeck's Fiction: The Aesthetics of the Road Taken.* Norman: U Oklahoma P, 1986.

Weber, Tom. *Cannery Row: A Time to Remember.* Monterey, CA: Orenda/Unity, 1983.

Whitebrook, Peter. *Staging Steinbeck: Dramatising "The Grapes of Wrath."* London: Cassell, 1988.

5: The 1990s: Visions

As SAID ABOVE, there is no handy line of demarcation between the 1980s and 1990s in Steinbeck criticism except the handy and lazy one of an accident of dating (as with the current millennial fever). Just as surely as those of us who can count to ten know that the new millennium starts in 2001, we acknowledge that 1990 was the last year of the 1980s. Each decade acquires its own retrospective coloration, but in these subjective terms a "decade" may not begin until three or four years along, and may also end as much later — or earlier. In Steinbeck studies, there is no clear delineation between decades possible; and in terms of all critical work, the same is true if only because the publications of the "new" decade, whenever it is felt to begin, reflect work in progress years before.

In 1990, three volumes of interest were published. One was issued under nominally British auspices, and its contributors, though Americans, were not Steinbeck specialists. The editor of *New Essays on "The Grapes of Wrath"* is David Wyatt, and his colleagues are Nellie Y. McKay, William Howarth, Stephen Railton, and Leslie Gossage. Wyatt's introduction is less a conventional preview of the essays that follow it than an independent fifth contribution to the book, focusing first on the novel's initial appearance and reception, and then on to what Wyatt sees as Steinbeck's revisionist presentation of the concept of "home" (encountered elsewhere in this survey):

> *The Grapes of Wrath* also marks the end of Steinbeck's conception of home as a place. The opening up of the family corresponds to a movement west in which the Joads discover the human power of indwelling. This is the power Tom invokes in his farewell speech, one he makes after finding that California will not provide his family a localized home. This promised land resists all attempts at entry, and so inspires, through its economic and geographical inaccessibility, a sublimation of the will to settle into citizenship in an immaterial domain of belonging. (Wyatt 19)

Wyatt concludes his introduction by invoking Milton — a strategy we have seen justified before. He is talking about Tom's patently Christlike promise to be with those in need always:

> This speech marks the culmination of Steinbeck's major phase. He has learned the value of home while losing belief in the possibility of it. . . . Tom appeals to the time-honored consolation for the loss of an earthly garden. (24)

Wyatt then reminds us of Milton's Michael's consolation of Adam to the effect that if he "adds love to faith, he will come to "possess/ A paradise within thee, happier far." Thus

> The beauty of the episode lies in the dreaming Eve's simultaneous incorporation of the promise, an act that enables her to voice, as she wakes to depart with her husband, the poem's radical insight about the relation of person to place. (24)

Wyatt concludes his poetically sensitive introduction by comparing Adam and Eve looking back to paradise "the way an Oklahoma family would one day look back at a receding home to see "the windows reddening under the first color of the sun." In both cases, Wyatt states, the characters learn that the place of rest which they seek lies in continuing motion:

> Walking becomes their destination and their destiny, and the world in which they seek "Their place of rest" resolves itself, not into a vale of privileged sites, but, in the last word of Milton's poem and the key word in Steinbeck's book, into a "way." (24)

This alone is worth the price of admission.

But it is not all. Besides Wyatt's and Gossage's essays (Gossage's is concerned with the Ford film version of the novel), we get: Stephen Railton's on "Steinbeck's Art of Conversion," which echoes Bunyan's *Pilgrim's Progress* as a way of viewing the Joads's journey towards change of heart; McKay's sturdy study of Ma Joad as presented in terms of role rather than individuality (one might welcome hearing an exchange on this subject between Nellie McKay and Mimi Gladstein); and another kind of mother in Howarth's study of journalism — that uniquely American preoccupation of many an American fictionist — as "The Mother of Literature." Much of this slim but illustrated book seems intended for persons just discovering the existence of Steinbeck's classic, yet it is fine to have some fresh voices on hand in the world of Steinbeck studies for a change. The book's subtitle is true and realized: these are indeed "new" essays.

Also in 1990, Jackson J. Benson published what was virtually his last hurrah as a Steinbeck critic. *The Short Novels of John Steinbeck: Critical Essays with a Checklist to Steinbeck Criticism* (the lengthy title tells one not to expect to buy this book at the airport departure lounge), is a volume that includes almost two dozen essays, many new to print. In addition to the six short works Viking Press had included in its 1953 volume *The Short Novels of John Steinbeck,* Benson adds what seemed at the time pariah numbers: *Burning Bright, Sweet Thursday,* and *The Short Reign of Pippin IV.* (For perhaps formalistic reasons, *The Pastures of Heaven* is excluded.)

As has been suggested above, Benson has never been known as a routine critical savage; he is as fair to his writers as he is to their work. The papers, many perhaps by now difficult to find in journal format, especially in libraries strapped for funds, are excellent overall and by no means exclusive as to subject matter. But characteristic of its genial editor is the pair of paragraphs near the ending of his introduction in which he imagines himself into the heart and soul of John Steinbeck, as most Steinbeck critics have. (And, as Jack Benson has in effect suggested, there is by now a community of Steinbeck critics who do not enjoy going after one another with crude, sharp weapons.) Benson turns his other cheek to the insolent critics of the cast by relegating their judgments to the pathetic biases of other spaces and times:

> Some may think of John Steinbeck as the great political writer of his time or — our most accomplished social novelist — observer and recorder of the farm family, the farm worker, and the Great Depression. But I am inclined to see him somewhat differently. He had witnessed and often shared great pain and suffering. The sight of Okie children needlessly starving or of workers being beaten by company thugs so paralyzed him with helpless anger that it was many months before he could approach the writing of his masterpiece with the detachment he needed. For almost two years after World War II he could not shake from his mind or his dreams the scenes of bloody pieces of women and children after bombardments in Italy. He had suffered much in his personal life, and he had endured more public abuse for his art than any man can rightly be asked to undergo: The day after he won the Nobel Prize for literature, the "newspaper of record," the *New York Times,* announced to the world in an editorial that he didn't deserve it.

But, as Benson sees Steinbeck's end times:

> Yet somehow he was always able to rise above his anger and pain. Near the end of his life I see him, "the great stage curtain about to drop," at his desk in his own little halfway house, Joyous Garde. He is writing. He does not stop to weep but plays out his scene. (Benson, *Short* 12–13)

Some subjects of biographies eventually inspire palpable dislike in their biographers. With all his human flaws, John Steinbeck has, as Benson imagines him at Sag Harbor, elicited poetry.

A listing of the contents and contributors to this still-useful volume, previously printed or not, should persuade the interested as to its value. *Tortilla Flat* is studied in terms of myth and philosophy by Joseph Fontenrose and Robert Gentry, respectively; Anne Loftis looks at the coming-to-be of *Of Mice and Men,* while William Goldhurst examines the "curse of Cain" in the same work and Mark Spilka considers the way the promise of Eden is shattered by violence.

Warren French compares *The Red Pony* in its story-cycle and film versions, while Howard Levant considers the book's narrative technique (in an article taken from a journal with that aspect as its special focus); Tetsumaro Hayashi and I look at *The Moon Is Down* in terms of the function of the character Dr. Winter and the play-novella's "Europeanness," again respectively; Peter Lisca's chapter from his second traversal of Steinbeck introduces *Cannery Row,* while Robert S. Hughes, Jr., contributes a chapter intriguingly entitled "Some Philosophers in the Sun" and a section of a prior Benson article looks into the work's place in the folk tradition.

As to *The Pearl,* John H. Timmerman sees Jungian patterns there, Michael J. Meyer sees it as a parable about "man's inescapable condition (172), while Roy S. Simmonds traces the work from a story Steinbeck heard in Mexico, to the film it became, and to the novel — a flawed one, as he sees it — the script was released as.

Charles R. Metzger places *Sweet Thursday* in the pastoral tradition, Louis Owens redeems its critical reputation as a "throwaway" novel by noting its positive aspects and concluding that it is nonetheless a "tour de force" (203), and Richard Astro notes the darker side of the supposedly saccharine work. For *Burning Bright,* the Carroll Britch-Clifford Lewis team work through Steinbeck's persistent motif of "shining" as the final vision of the protagonist Joe Saul, and Mimi R. Gladstein looks at both it and *Sweet Thursday* as examples of what she calls "straining for profundity."

Finally, Owens (again) looks at *The Short Reign of Pippin IV* and rightly argues that it is about not contemporary France but "America and the relation between private and public morality" (256) and that it failed to be perceived as anything but a lighthearted satirical romp. And a section of Levant's book examines (of course) the work's structure.

Just as the volume was prefaced by Steinbeck's essay on his shorter works, it is completed by an "overview" by Robert Morsberger on the history of Steinbeck's association with the stage.

In the same year, John H. Timmerman issued a fleshed-out version of his previous study of the short fiction, *The Dramatic Landscape of Steinbeck's Short Stories.* This time, Timmerman traces patterns in the development of the writer as a short-story artist, a career perhaps unnecessarily curtailed by the market demands and realities in existence towards the end of Steinbeck's career.

Timmerman shrewdly observes Steinbeck's method in the stories of *The Long Valley*:

> . . . Steinbeck's storytelling method belies his nonteleological premises. One may also observe a deepening awareness of the artist's task to rearrange observed experience in Steinbeck's letters. It is clear, for example, that the drama of the migrant workers was so compelling to Steinbeck at this time that he believed the simple act of exposing their situation was sufficient. Their story needed no adumbration by didactic exhortations. His task as a writer was to get that story, as cleanly and powerfully as his talent permitted. (Timmerman 237)

Timmerman's thorough study leads him to a conclusion apparently unavailable to other scholars, except perhaps for "Chip" Hughes: that the stories, different in form and requisites as they are from the novels, were in fact the proving grounds for the latter genre:

> The short stories were a proving ground for ideas and themes, but also for skills. If the imagery patterns sometimes seemed to acquire a life of their own and virtually dominate the story, Steinbeck was learning the complex revelation of theme through image. One sees this fulfilled in the late novels also, in the serpentine imagery of the temptress Cathy Ames, for example. Steinbeck is duly noted as one of America's great orchestrators of imagery patterns, and the complex patterns in such works as *East of Eden, The Pearl,* and *The Winter of Our Discontent* were proven first in the short stories. (284)

Many have written on Steinbeck's whole body of work and even more have written on individual short stories, but only Hughes and Timmerman have looked at the latter as, in effect, a single body of work with its own temporally sustained legitimacy and applied that body of work, and its inherent values, to the more famous and longer Steinbeck titles.

On Steinbeckian second thought, as in the narrational voice employed in *East of Eden,* there does seem to be a natural break between the decades of the eighties and nineties. Precious little appeared at the start of the nineties, yet both a newer and an older generation seemed to gather up steam not far into the era.

Like the Edinburgh production of a few years before (see previous chapter), Frank Galati's Steppenwolf Theatre Company's stage production of *The Grapes of Wrath* was staged in Great Britain (before coming to New York for a successful Broadway run). Even earlier, it had been developed at Steppenwolf's home base in Chicago and then also put on in La Jolla. Eventually it was taped for showing on PBS (the American Public Broadcasting System). Illusions such as rain, a flowing stream, and the movements of the family truck were especially telling on a largely bare stage. The cast was larger than Whitebrook's, and the production is ideally suited for a university-level (i.e., a large non-professional scale) company. (For instance, it was later given a memorable traversal by Detroit's Wayne State University Hilberry Company.)

Galati's text differs from Whitebrook's in that it is not a journal, but just about anything a company would want or have to know before attempting its own run. This includes notes on lighting, costumes, blocking, props, etc. But of chief interest here is the adaptation of Steinbeck's text, always faithful to its spirit and often grittier than the novel was allowed to be on first publication in 1939. Though Steinbeck's masterwork has not yet been turned into an opera — as *Of Mice and Men* and *Burning Bright* have — such a development may be only a matter of time, as cabaret performer Michael Smith's apposite, folkish score (sung onstage) suggests. However, it does not seem appropriate to attempt to deal with the details of a stage production here, especially one so able to stand on its own. Serious studies of the adaptation have to date scarcely begun.

Sparky Enea was a surviving member of the crew of the *Western Flyer,* on which Steinbeck, Ed Ricketts, and five others (including Steinbeck's first wife, Carol) voyaged to the Sea of Cortez, resulting in a memorable joint philosophical and marine-biological report, which was printed the year after the 1940 adventure. In 1990, Enea published his memoirs, *With Steinbeck in the Sea of Cortez,* and these are fascinatingly illustrated. Enea was almost the sole survivor of a generation of Steinbeck buddies with a particularly local axe to grind — no, make that a simple understandable longing for times past when their bodies performed on cue and their pals were all together. Enea is moving when he describes the days after the war in which he became a local bartender and gave Steinbeck's few letters to him away to "young soldiers." There is an especial sadness to his lack of physical contact with the writer in later years — and Enea's book was dictated when he was eighty! From thousands of miles from his subject and decades of time, he rationalizes their failures to get in real touch in a way that puts him on a level with the writer and blames the latter for the implicit snub:

> . . . maybe John had changed. I saw those pictures of him in the Salinas Library with his third wife, Elaine. My God — suits, ties, overcoats and even a tuxedo when he got the Nobel Prize. I had never seen him in anything but levis and an old seaman's cap. So that's probably why I never saw him again. He was a completely different kind of guy. (Enea 69)

This is sad, but understandable: "suits, ties, overcoats" were to blame for exiling Sparky Enea, who was uncomprehending.

Editor Audry Lynch must have had her hands full editing the interview tapes for this "as told to" volume of memories, but to the Steinbeckian it is full of color and interest. Enea had for years proved a candid and willing performer at annual summer Steinbeck festivals in Steinbeck's home town of Salinas, and the best of his yarns are gathered here. This volume is primarily of biographical interest, but undeniably so.

Undeniably a maverick volume, Donald V. Coers's *John Steinbeck as Propagandist: "The Moon Is Down" Goes to War* was issued in 1991, and is to date the only entire book of criticism devoted to that title. *Moon* is unquestionably a watershed publication in Steinbeck's career, since it marks his departure from the strictures of Ed Ricketts's notions of the "group man" of the 1930s and towards the idea of an independent and unconditioned individualistic homo sapiens.

Coers's study shows how the play-novella managed to attract the attention of the citizens of the occupied nations, regardless of any preconceptions they might naturally have brought to the reading of the book. In the mid-forties, the United States issued a series of "Occupied Nations" postage stamps, the first to be printed privately and in multiple colors. The series was not without flaws, but it eventually touched the citizens of the countries affected, and Steinbeck's book performed the same function.

Coers's strategy is to begin with the "American Reception" of *The Moon Is Down,* and then go on to the very different response to be found in the Nazi-occupied countries which had had, after all, a truer look at the realities of the German presence.

With respect to the home-audience reception of the book, Coers notes that "Steinbeck had emerged as the preeminent proletarian novelist of his day. Suddenly the publication of his first novel since *The Grapes of Wrath* brought criticism which questioned not only his skill as a writer but also — and far worse — his credentials as an antifascist, his political instincts, and his very patriotism" (Coers 22).

Things were very different where the occupation was actually in effect. Coers devotes a chapter apiece to Norway, where the play-novella presumably takes place, Denmark, the Netherlands, France, and "Other Countries," such as Sweden and Switzerland — neutral states surrounded by captive ones — and even the Soviet Union where, curiously, critics tended to be negative, paralleling the situation in the United States, but for vastly different reasons: "Official Nazi racial policy had designated the Russian people *Untermenschen*, or subhumans, and Nazi soldiers, accordingly, had brutalized the populace" (120). Anyone who has visited sites where German soldiers carried out deliberately destructive and gratuitous assaults on the evidence of the existence of Russian — and Polish — culture can agree with Coers's conclusion: "Small wonder that in a land where German atrocities were committed on an inconceivable scale, Steinbeck's 'Nazi' invaders seemed airy figments of a naive foreigner's imagination" (120). Coers finishes by adding that *The Moon Is Down* performed useful service for the Chinese who were even more brutalized at the hands of the Japanese.

Coers refers, towards the end of his presentation, to the vast number of foreign editions of *Moon* that have appeared since the War — by 1989, "some seventy-six editions" (136). These include several in British and American English, Danish, Dutch, Spanish (in Spain, Mexico, South America), Hungarian, French (in France and Belgium), Turkish, German (in Switzerland), Chinese, Japanese, Arabic, Swedish, Italian, Portuguese (in Portugal and Brazil), Korean, Urdu (in India), Greek, Polish, Farsi (in Iran), Burmese, Norwegian (of course), and Slovak (Coers's source surely errs in ascribing this one to Yugoslavia, 136).

Coers concludes that while *Moon* is clearly "not among Steinbeck's best novels," but rather an "unassuming work whose transparency of purpose makes it particularly vulnerable to criticism in our age of sophisticated metafiction" (138). Yet

> . . . To readers affected most directly by the terror and despair of Nazi occupation, *The Moon Is Down* was an inspiriting statement of faith that despite the darkness of their hour, freedom and decency would return. That power to inspire — its greatest virtue for millions of victims of Nazi oppression — remains today its signal distinction. After the lights had gone out all over Europe for the second time in our

century, John Steinbeck's modest novel was a beacon of hope in a seemingly hopeless night. (138)

Coers's use of "modest" to describe *The Moon Is Down* is apt, for he means it in no derogatory way, and he likely would not object to having it applied to his own admittedly specialized study of such a work. For while Steinbeck critics had for decades been alluding to the reputation of *Moon* abroad, especially at the time it was written, no one had really made the effort to sleuth out the evidence for the effect the book had on foreign audiences, particularly those in the occupied countries. Coers has turned assumptions into reliable knowledge.

A laid-back southerner in no mood to hurry, Donald R. Noble published the 1989 Tuscaloosa *Steinbeck Question* papers in 1993, but the publisher, Whitston, did right by the extremely varied essays contributed. The seventeen pieces have little in common but routine competence and even excellence. Critics of some reputation were on hand, and also a number previously unheard from. (Those who were not in attendance may find this anthology a particularly rich one. Those who were there may also savor the recollections of suburban Alabama barbequed ribs.) In either case, Tuscaloosa proved to be a unique and unprecedented conference venue and topic. Whatever on earth "the Steinbeck Question" finally meant, or means, this result of the increasingly desperate search for new conference topics managed to be an enormous success — however unlikely it might have seemed at the start.

In fact, conference participants perhaps were unsure of just what the "Steinbeck question" was beforehand, but instead of asking "What is it?" decided to go and make their visit(s). Noble attempts, in what is perhaps an a posteriori fashion, to suggest in his introduction that there are in fact many questions or "conundrums" about Steinbeck (and thus, that maybe Steinbeck is himself the question). Why, for instance "has Steinbeck not received the intense academic scrutiny awarded his peers?" (Noble 2). Why is such a politically committed person such as Steinbeck the "darling" of neither the Left nor the Right? Have some works simply failed to get their share of attention, or been misinterpreted to date? The latter is surely a rhetorical question to which these conference papers are gestures at answering (2–3).

Noble goes on to preview, one by one, the papers included, which are arranged both chronologically (in terms of the Steinbeck canon) and thematically. They are framed by essays by Jackson J. Benson and John H. Timmerman. Benson asks the question of why Steinbeck managed to elicit so much critical and community hostility over his career and concludes that after bucking a general Eastern prejudice towards things Western, he seemed to abandon the West. There is also the matter of his politics, and, interestingly, his use of supposedly profane language in a censorious era (at least so far as the schools are concerned) but also his use of humor, which leads some to dismiss him as fundamentally unserious. At the book's end, Timmerman views Steinbeck as a "shameless magpie" (as the writer called himself) unafraid to honestly borrow from his wide reading.

Dennis Prindle traces what he calls "allegorical naturalism" through the early fictions, while Robert S. Hughes includes his essay on "Steinbeck and the Art of Story Writing." Charlotte Hadella studies a phenomenon she finds pervasive in (especially) the early works, the "cloistered woman." Paul Hintz zeroes in on a different aspect of the same syndrome: the "silent woman" in a *Cannery Row* dominated by a male voice, or voices:

> We are left with an unresolved contradiction: the World as thing, as other. The Other as object, the subject the Male Author, in control of the process of naming. . . . (81)

To Mimi Gladstein, women are not only cloistered and silent, but they are also simply "missing" — that is, for a writer who knew so many extraordinary women (not simply including his three wives), there are precious few even resembling that level of intelligence and attainment in his writings. This fleshes out the argument adumbrated in her book-length study, that it is in effect easier to turn womankind into symbols of indestructibility than to understand them as fully developed characters.

Michael J. Meyer, who appears to love Genesis as much as Steinbeck did, has another go at "The Snake" in terms of its "fallen Adam" protagonist. Michael G. Barry offers an essay entitled "Degrees of Mediation and Their Political Value," by which he means the tug upon the Joads to adopt a theoretical political panacea for their plight:

> A choice needs to be made, and so Steinbeck offers us socialism, the system in which the migrants will be required to sacrifice the unity of the family in order to attain or hope for some greater unity which will topple the existing order; they are to look ahead toward a better time when they have won their battle, rather than look down at their feet, and perhaps plan dinner for the evening. (111)

But, as Sylvia J. Cook states in her essay, "Steinbeck's Poor in Prosperity and Adversity," which ends with Thoreau's *Walden* as context for her study of Steinbeck's have-nots, the latter seem to have a quality that posits hope:

> Although many of the qualities which Steinbeck emphasizes in his poor people are distinctly mental ones, what has been more often noted in them is a dionysiac element in their behavior that encompasses ready violence, drunkenness and sensuality, and thus might seem to vindicate the common sense of them as primitives. However, their violence is almost invariably linked to a sense of justice that is either highly personal or in direct opposition to the injustice they see practiced in society. (138)

And in a tour de force that included musical performance at the conference, Steinbeck is compared in terms of subject matter and societal impact to Woody Guthrie by H. R. Stoneback.

Noble's stable of critics now turns to the nonfiction. In an intriguingly entitled essay, "Patterns of Reality and Barrels of Worms," Louis Owens moves from *Sea of Cortez* to *Travels with Charley* in showing how the writer's tendency to plan his accounts before the experiences were in place led to inevitable disappointment:

> . . . Undertaking an undeniably courageous quest but sadly overburdened with preconceptions and pre-established patterns, on this journal Steinbeck found only his own barrel of worms. . . . by the time he came to write *Travels with Charley,* Steinbeck's world had narrowed, his enthusiasm and interest dulled with age as he predicted until, finally, he did indeed retire into easy didacticism. (181)

Robert E. Morsberger delivers a historical account of Steinbeck's experiences in the war, while Alan Brown's short paper claims that writing *Bombs Away* lowered Steinbeck's sights from those of an "artist" to those of a "craftsman."

In a two-essay section on Steinbeck's dramatic writing, I look at *Burning Bright* not in terms of fiction but those of the work's inherent and defensible theatricality. Jeremy G. Butler interestingly contrasts the period of the Mexican Revolution with the era of HUAC (the House Un-American Activities Committee), when Steinbeck prepared the screenplay for *Viva Zapata!* Finally, Charles L. Etheridge, Jr., surveys changing attitudes towards Steinbeck's "naturalism" and his *East of Eden* in recent years, this writer being among a list of subjects also including Peter Copek, Benson, DeMott, and Timmerman. All in all, as is obvious, this was a conference loaded with riches, and its printed proceedings are of enduring value.

The term "revisions" begins to make sense when one considers Warren French's 1989 *John Steinbeck's Fiction Revisited,* a volume that wholly recasts his previous TUSAS (Twayne's United States Authors Series) title from the 1960s, which incidentally had already been replaced by another series title in 1975. Warren French has always been as easy on his feet as a skilled basketball player, and the remarkable fact about this World War II veteran is that he refuses to sit pat in a foxhole. He continues to rethink his positions and recast his approaches to Steinbeck. By the time of the publication of this book, Warren French was not about to be bossed around by a series editor. His volume is original and heartfelt.

This was to be French's third go at writing summary criticism of Steinbeck's major works, and once again he is more willing than most writers to change his mind. He refers to his second attempt succinctly, framing it initially in terms of what he had tried to accomplish in his revised or second edition of 1974:

> . . . Although at that time of a review of national priorities after the American involvement in Vietnam some commentators, including Steinbeck's son John, spoke of him as "the conscience of America," I argued that during a period when there was great concern about consciousness-raising in personal and political affairs he might more accurately be perceived as producing "dramas of consciousness," employing a phrase originated by Henry James in his preface to the New York edition of his early novel *Roderick Hudson.* (French, *Revisited* ix)

Steinbeck's son John struggled mightily to maintain an even perspective on his father as a personal and public figure during the son's shortened life, but one senses that French's slant on the son's point of view was an apt one. Yet who else but French would have thought to connect the Californian fictionist to, of all people, Henry James?

French fixes upon Steinbeck's frustrating ability to inspire a readership even late into a century about to expire. He is kinder to Bloom's editions than has been the case in these pages, perhaps out of simple respect (x). Chapters that deal with such disparate topics as "Searching for a Folk Hero" bring together Steinbeck titles rarely if ever discussed at all.

Interestingly, even though French does not seem willing to entertain, as others have, the notion of Steinbeck in his later years as a "postmodernist," he seems fascinated by the idea of the writer as in search of "a hero equal to the challenge of the times," meaning post-

World War II (36). His conclusion to this chapter seems, considering his preconceptions, eminently just:

> . . . This is not to say that authors should continue, against their own artistic impulses, to write as they have earlier, though some supporters may urge this course. All one can say is that authors should be remembered for their best work, and Steinbeck did it during the disillusioning decades after World War I, before World War II introduced a nuclear age. Speculations about his "decline," though they cannot be avoided, because he persisted beyond his prime, are really beside the point. Whatever may have been the reasons, it appears to have been inevitable. We should be concerned with the legacy he left us, not with what we probably did not miss. (37)

It is hard to see what a critic weaned on naturalism, realism, and modernism might have done better in the way of a critical updating of John Steinbeck's fiction.

In 1996, French also "reconsidered" Steinbeck's nonfiction, but in fact this was a first separate treatment of the subject. This may also have been a commercially risky title for Twayne to attempt to market, given its almost university library/student orientation. *John Steinbeck's Nonfiction Revisited* deals with a vast range of work by a writer who among others tried to be more than a fictionist.

French quotes Arthur Miller as "the person who appears to have best understood Steinbeck" when the playwright met the novelist, who had just moved to New York:

> I think what John suffered was really a personal thing. We have an urban civilization, and John was not an urban man. He liked to think he was sometimes. . . . And I think one of John's problems is the same as mine or anyone else's in this country or maybe in this world where there is no continuity, or very much community. He was trying to find a community in the United States that would feed him, towards which he could react in a feeling way, rather than merely as an observer or a commentator. And I don't know if there is such a place left in the world. (French, quoting Miller, *Nonfiction* xiii)

What French calls Miller's "sensitive perception" mirrors those of Miller himself in his own works as well as those of Steinbeck; but it applies perfectly well to French's own kinds of sensitive perceptions. One cannot but help react towards Miller's crucial word, "feed," in terms of which Steinbeck himself is a type of that desperate man at the end of *The Grapes of Wrath* in need of nourishment of whatever sort. The pathos of this terminology still applied to the writer himself.

French is tantalizing when he cites the need to see Steinbeck's last fictions, *The Short Reign of Pippin IV* and *The Winter of Our Discontent*, in the light of the uncollected pieces, largely untranslated, that Steinbeck contributed to the Paris *Le Figaro* in 1954. French picks up on his opening Miller quote to say that here Steinbeck reveals what French calls his "Lone Ranger" side, that is, the writer who wanders off alone, the better to criticize a community he feels ethically estranged from. French concludes:

> It was this acceptance of the uniqueness of his personal vision that carried Steinbeck through his two final novels. Pippin IV prepares to give up for good his position in Paris and his overwhelming responsibility for decisions that the people did not really want him to make. Ethan Allen Hawley realizes in *The Winter of Our Discontent* that his responsibility is not to a corrupted wasteland community but to his daughter, to whom he must return the family talisman, "lest another light go out."
>
> These are not Steinbeck's most effective novels, and he did not devote the rest of his life to this isolated vision; but it supported him through what proved one of the happiest periods of his personal life until he sallied forth to rediscover his country and found it in need of following a new path that it had not found. The *Figaro* papers chart Steinbeck's course as he begins to find a new way of his own, and they need to be read in the context of his day-to-day thoughts as he gropes for a path toward a sense of personal peace from 1954 to 1960, when in the course of his travels to rediscover the United States, as T. S. Eliot puts it at the end of "The Love Song of J. Alfred Prufrock," human voices wake him and he drowns. (128–29)

French ends his volume with an unusual deserved "Personal Note" wherein he draws attention to the persistence of the Arthurian sense of *comitatus* in the later Steinbeck: "The critics were the outsiders . . . seeking to destroy the comradeship of good fellows" (131). French finishes by dealing with the "inconsistencies" in Steinbeck's attitudes:

> . . . He did have a tendency toward the metaphysical, especially in its gaudier manifestations, which colored his fiction more than his reporting, but which did lead him away from addressing tough issues to allegorizing. Let us ride into the sunset with the Lone Ranger image that I have been belaboring, contemplating that John Steinbeck's fictions were his many masks and speculating how much he unmasked in his nonfiction. (131–32)

French's slight self-indulgence provides a generous tone of open-endedness in this thorough and necessary volume that is unlikely to be surpassed for some long time to come — if ever.

The year 1995 produced a series title akin to Louis Owens's from the same press, Twayne, earlier on, and by something of an Owens disciple: Charlotte Cook Hadella's *"Of Mice and Men": A Kinship of Powerlessness.*

Hadella does not overburden this classic novella with more critical weight than it can bear, much as it has taken on over the years. In six short chapters, plus notes and a bibliography, she manages to come in under a hundred pages. Hadella includes a chapter on screen versions of the work, though not its operatic one.

Given her subtitle, Hadella steers closely to her chosen and self-restricted theme. She observes:

> In *Of Mice and Men*, Steinbeck features just such an "unhappy fraternity": barley buckers, a bunkhouse hand, a mule skinner, a stable buck, and a lonely woman. These characters are thrust into conflict with the ranch owner, his son, and a social structure that views them more as expendable commodities than as worthwhile human beings. They are challenged to discover and to maintain their humanity in the fact of overwhelmingly dehumanizing forces. In this sense, their story is not just an American drama that takes place in a particular region of the country at a particular time in history; it is a human drama for all places and all times. (Hadella 7)

Aside from her penchant for Bakhtin-quoting, Hadella's reading of the play-novella is a traditional one, as when she concludes — in a chapter before considering the stage and film versions of the work — that

> . . . By killing Lennie, George consciously decides to give his friend the only protection available to him. With the fatal pistol shot, George rationalizes that he has sent Lennie off to the dream farm forever. By the time George walks away from the grove with Slim, he has let go of the escape dream for himself as well and has embraced the competing dream of living without Lennie and just being one of the guys. Though Steinbeck lets the reader decide which George speaks through the pistol — the one who creates the world of protected innocence or the one who expresses a desire for freedom trigger is a reaction to the voices of a cruel reality from which neither he nor Lennie can escape any longer. (63)

If Hadella seems to have at first convicted George of selfish action, then, she also voices (in the end) his human dilemma as an insufferable one that involves a sacrifice of a wild creature's limb. And thus did the critics of the most recent era manage to evade the traps set out for them by series publishers.

Also in 1995, Brian E. Railsback published a revised version of his doctoral dissertation, *Parallel Expeditions: Charles Darwin and the Art of John Steinbeck.* No scholar had done more than allude to Darwin in connection to Steinbeck before, and Railsback's full-length study, though not pleasing all critics, breaks new ground that obviously was asking for plowing. Early on in his treatise, he states his overall judgment:

> Darwin and evolutionary theory hover over the books Steinbeck read at a crucial period in his development as a writer; sometimes Darwin is debated or questioned, but more often he is revered. His name appears again and again and is linked with evolution in a revolutionary perspective, that view of the world that underlines the power of inductive, objective reasoning — a holistic understanding which successfully challenges preconceptions. That linking of Darwin to so much of what Steinbeck admired as well as the fascination the novelist had for evolutionary progress and natural selection helps to explain why . . . Darwin's name comes up most often in *The Log From the Sea of Cortez.* (Railsback 25)

Railsback frames his volume, or bookends it, with references to two conference addresses. He opens with the 1989 keynote address Leslie Fiedler delivered in San Jose, noting how he called Steinbeck "a middlebrow author for middlebrow critics" in front of a number of prominent Steinbeck critics of whose existence he seemed either unaware or contemptuous. In spite of an obviously "irritated" audience, Fiedler seemed quite proud of manipulating his celebrity's presence to display his ignorance (1), which Railsback politely refers to as "the legacy of critical misinterpretation summarized by Leslie Fiedler's 1989 speech" (12). As implied earlier, "critical ignorance" might have been more accurate, since there was precious little evidence in his 1989 performance that Fiedler had read any Steinbeck critics, or even Steinbeck, in a terribly long time.

Railsback finishes with a pleasanter recollection of a brilliant tour de force of a lecture given in 1992 at the Nantucket "Steinbeck and the Environment" Conference by the late Professor Stanley Brodwin of Hofstra University. To an audience of scientists and critics and environmentalists, Brodwin covered turf common to all disciplines represented and left the old Admiral Coffin School hall "filled with applause," after which the invigorated assembly "ambled up the cobbled roads into Nantucket Village with the author's wife near the head of the group." "It was a good day for Steinbeck studies . . . Had he been there, John Steinbeck would have been pleased" (138–39). Railsback and the others were thus pleased, and not only because they had listened to someone who knew what he was talking about.

Typical of Railsback's methods is a summary judgment of *Grapes of Wrath* in Darwinian terms, but they scarcely become overly technical to the point of obscuring the novel itself:

> In a work so full of apparently hopeless suffering, the Darwinian view of *The Grapes of Wrath* explains why characters such as Ma or Tom have a sense of victory. The processes of competition and natural selection, artificially heightened by narrow-minded landowners, create a new race with strong blood — a race that can adapt and fight in a way the old one could not. Endowed with a closeness to the land and an increasing sympathy, this new race represents a human being far superior to the old "I" savage. Because of the struggle, people like the Joads become better human beings, cooperating with each other in every crisis. "There is a gradual improvement in the treatment of man by man," Steinbeck wrote . . . "There are little spots of kindness that burn up like fire and burn the whole thing up. But I guess the reason they are so bright is that there are so few of them. However, the ones that do burn up seem to push us ahead a little.". . . (137–38)

Railsback is, of course, speaking of the evolutionary improvement of the human heart. His book remains of permanent interest as a first specialized study of an aspect of Steinbeck heretofore taken, like so many others, for granted.

The same year saw the publication of the second major biography of John Steinbeck: Jay Parini's plainly titled *John Steinbeck: A Biography*. Parini, a writer of fiction, poetry, and criticism, seemed at first to be an odd choice to take on the Californian, but he had help from both Elaine Steinbeck and the Steinbeck Research Center at San Jose, as is evident in the previously unpublished photographs that are included. For reasons never understood by this writer, the work was first published in England and came here equipped with an unusual set of local encomia: blurbs from abroad to sell books in America.

Parini's volume took him four years to write, less than half of the time Jackson Benson spent on his; and adjusting for the difference in typeface size, it can be called little more than half as long. It fleshes out the period of the 1940s to the end of Steinbeck's life notably, probably again the result of consultations with Steinbeck's widow. It includes some suggestions about the writer's relationships that would seem mere gossip in our present context.

Parini's preface includes a judicious, then modest, assessment of his predecessors' work:

> While Kiernan's book is insubstantial and, quite often, inaccurate, Professor Benson's important book has proven invaluable to me. He interviewed many of the people who knew Steinbeck personally, and since most of these are now dead, his work is an indispensable gift to all admirers of John Steinbeck and to all future biographers. (Parini xx)

True enough: While Benson was by no means intentionally recording witnesses at the ends of their lives, his volume was in retrospect an incomparably fortuitously timed venture that Parini's or any yet to come cannot hope to match. Yet Parini shrewdly makes distinctions in his own epilogue that make his approach seem newly of its time.

For instance, he asserts of Steinbeck that "he did not write in the tradition of modernism, which has been the focus of most academic inquiry; he did, however, absorb many of the techniques of modernism, diverting them to his own purposes while cultivating an almost childlike simplicity" that gives conventional critics apparently little to do. After a decade or two of work by other hands, it was now safe to simply presume that Steinbeck was not a "modernist." And, he notes, "More subtly, the mythopoeic approach of his later work confused readers who continued to judge this work by the standards of social realism typical of his novels in the late thirties" (488).

The item in Parini's biography that aroused the most interest when the book first appeared, especially since the work as a whole was issued with the apparent blessing of Elaine Steinbeck, the novelist's third wife, tended initially to verge on sensationalism masked as reportage: the revelation that Steinbeck had demanded that a pregnant Carol (his first wife) undergo an abortion because he was too preoccupied as a writer to be a father:

> . . . But what was in the marriage for Carol without children, especially now that her intimacy with Steinbeck was threatened by the breakdown in their relations? The marital crisis intensified when, just after Christmas, Carol discovered that she was pregnant. Steinbeck panicked, insisting that she get an abortion, and she finally agreed to go through with it against her better judgment. Unfortunately, an infection developed in the uterine tubes that led, within months, to a complete hysterectomy: an utterly devastating operation for a woman of childbearing age who wanted a child very badly. As might be expected, Carol never got over the bitterness of this. The situation was made infinitely worse by the fact that her marriage was dissolving

right under her, although at this time she did not anticipate the full extent of her problems. (Parini 227)

Parini tries, in fairness to Steinbeck, to explain his actions in terms of his insecurities, and his awareness that Carol was an especially strong woman:

> . . . One consequence of this fear was an inability to read Carol's motives or affect objectively. He also distrusted his talent enough to worry about losing it, and he may have believed that Carol's "demands" on him, and the needs of any children who might come along, would sink the fragile craft of his fiction. (228)

Perhaps so. But Steinbeck took his bad conscience with him into his affair with second wife Gwyn, who bore him two sons but who also taunted him with the Strindbergian possibility that they might not be Steinbeck's; and so Parini's insert is not merely tabloid stuff but of real critical impact, coloring as it does all subsequent depictions of relations between husband and wife and parent and child in the later works, particularly *Burning Bright* and *The Winter of Our Discontent*.

Almost sixty years had elapsed before such clear-cut judgments could be safely made. Parini has his own favorite works, of course, noting that *"The Red Pony* must sleep uneasily on the library shelf beside *The Wayward Bus"* — the cayuse apparently being preferable to the clunker — and he is notably kind to *The Winter of Our Discontent*. Parini's final paragraph summons for praise, as if on awards night, not only Steinbeck's "compassion and lyrical precision," but also his prophetic concern for the "biosphere" and the "environment" (488). Managing to make pertinent commentary on the works as he moves along and yet attend as well to the calendar, Parini's biography achieves its own sort of permanent value.

In a sense, the next entry — a decidedly major one — might well have served as the final entry in our third chapter. It is *After "The Grapes of Wrath": Essays on John Steinbeck in Honor of Tetsumaro Hayashi*. And while Hayashi is represented literally only by means of a lengthy checklist of his work (compiled by one of the editors, Robert DeMott) and a portrait, he is the honored presence that animates its pages, both as the guiding and energizing force behind most of the scholars who are gathered inside, and also as a natural result, the object of their tribute. All those over the years who felt his presence even outside of the Steinbeck Society conspired to make this volume a reality.

That much having been said, it ought to be noted that the volume is a delight to hold and read, and it was handsomely printed by the Ohio

University (where DeMott teaches) Press, with some assistance from the staff of Sam Houston State University in Texas, where the other two editors, Donald V. Coers and Paul D. Ruffin, teach.

These essays are a deliberately mixed bag as regards direction, and their choice seems to have been made largely on grounds of the need to show the burgeoning variety in Steinbeck studies in the 1990s. Warren French is again on hand to provide an introduction — and a sense of overall control, but he also gracefully acknowledges Hayashi's place in the history of the movement he did so much to fuel. French is also a master at showing each essay's merits without shying away from showing how many could have been made even stronger.

French does allude (Coers, *After* 16) to his own ability to shift his positions, something mentioned here earlier on. Indeed, it has been characteristic of Steinbeck critics — at least those who have stayed the course and remained current in their reading — that they have not only been open to the possibility of changing their own opinions (or, should we say, the healthy necessity), but that they have been uncommonly willing to listen to their colleagues and to admit to having learned from them.

For example, Robert DeMott has always been such a critic. But in the present collection of essays, he finds opportunity to praise Louis Owens's willingness to change:

> Louis Owens's change of tune about *East of Eden* can be considered a trope for this current trend toward re-evaluating Steinbeck's novel in a positive light and for considering the book — among many other possibilities — as a postmodernist creation or metafictional construct. . . . Owens's insistence in *Re-Vision* that *East of Eden* can only be analyzed as an objective product has changed drastically. (152)

And he goes on to make his observation more specific still:

> In three overlapping essays (in 1989, 1990, and 1993) Louis Owens has focused his attention on *East of Eden* as a processive construct and a self-conscious fiction, aspects far more congenial to understanding the dynamics of Steinbeck's complicated effort in narrative form and characterization than the blueprint methods of earlier criticism. (153)

Of course, a few critics (including DeMott) had been suggesting as much for some time.

As suggested in an earlier chapter with respect to clarity of style, it is possible that Steinbeck's openness to innovation has proved infectious among his critics as well. Certainly that spirit has been embodied in his widow Elaine, who has generously acted the role of muse at many a

Steinbeck gathering. Editor Coers concludes the text section of the book with a lengthy interview with Elaine Steinbeck, fascinating especially for her firsthand recollections of the Steinbecks' lives together.

The earlier two sections of the volume are divided, necessarily arbitrarily but accurately enough, into the topics "General Essays" and "Essays on Specific Works." Familiar and unfamiliar presences grace the latter, which contains eleven pieces by Roy S. Simmonds, Eiko Shiraga, Kevin Hearle, Debra K. S. Barker, Brian Railsback, John Ditsky, DeMott (two contributions: a "straight" essay on *Sweet Thursday;* and an annotated "bibliographical survey" of *East of Eden*), Michael Meyer (on the Cain theme in *The Winter of Our Discontent,* the beginning of an edition of essays on Cain figures in Steinbeck, forthcoming), Geralyn Strecker, and Mimi Gladstein. Only *The Wayward Bus* and *The Moon Is Down* get more than one essay.

The first section has a most interesting account by Cliff Lewis of Steinbeck's involvement with politics in the FDR era, a piece on "Steinbeck and Ethnicity" by Susan Shillinglaw, and the usual thoroughly detailed account (this time on Steinbeck motion picture film scores) by Robert Morsberger. In the second section, and since we have just been looking at his own book, Brian Railsback contributes a paper entitled *"The Wayward Bus:* Misogyny or Sexual Selection?," which indicates that of course he sees the novel as right up his alley of specialized interest. He concludes:

> *The Wayward Bus,* as harsh a view of *Homo sapiens* as in *In Dubious Battle,* most fully extends Steinbeck's biological perspective into human sexual relations. The novel is a grotesque portrayal of Darwin's theory of sexual selection, made all the more distressing because of the repression and perversion of sex by a warped society. The characters are coldly measured by their control over biological reality. The better people understand their desires. Juan and Mildred meet in a barn, satiate their needs, and play at romance until they both know the game is over. Camille Oaks sees the sexual power plays of society for what they are, and she knows the role her body and the men around her have forced her to play. Norma believes in the romantic pap of Hollywood movies, but she also possesses a toughness to face reality, to face the grotesque, when it reaches out to grab her. Elliot and Bernice Pritchard wrap themselves in the lies of middle-class respectability, and when the truth of their own sexual power game appears in a cave, they scurry to deny what they see. Alice and Van Brunt live in a waning physical world; as their bodies run down, the fear of their mortality possesses them. Pimples is disfigured, undesirable, but is so base in his nature he is little better than the fly Stein-

beck has made him. *The Wayward Bus* is meant to be a slap in the face, but certainly not just for women. Rather, it attacks the inherent weakness of a society that has gone Hollywood, that has tried to cover up biological reality with make-up, booze, or a handsome business suit. (133–34)

Remembering the Parini material and the sampling of Railsback's study just attended to, we can see how originally such new matter can contribute to the defense of one of Steinbeck's pariah titles. But this is only a taste of the enormous diversity of approaches represented in this valuable volume. With such fresh attention being given to less often considered Steinbeck titles, *After "The Grapes of Wrath"* is both a necessary acquisition and an appropriate tribute to the legacy of Tetsumaro Hayashi.

Of somewhat lesser importance, by design, and by now perhaps difficult to locate, is a monograph issued in 1996. The annual Brown-Forman Classics in Context Festival at the celebrated Actors Theatre of Louisville turned to *East of Eden* as the year's dramatic project, and Joel A. Smith edited the more academic side of the proceedings as *Steinbeck on Stage & Film*. Aside from publicity pieces on company and festival, there is a very brief "journal" account by Alan Cook on the adaptor's role, and formal lectures by Jay Parini and Porter Anderson — the latter on "The Very American Theatricality of John Steinbeck." Anderson is an editor for CNN, the Cable News Network, out of Atlanta. He is a former theater critic and, of course, currently a journalist. But his piece on the theatricality of John Steinbeck is full in its scope and thorough in its research. He wonders aloud at the small number of "volunteer" audience members at Broadway plays, that is, people who seek out a particular show and willingly attend it, and he poses a rhetorical question which he answers at once:

> How, then, does the Steinbeck oeuvre, being made of far better stuff than the usual mass appeal, draw so many "volunteers"?
> My intuition tells me that the answer has to do with insecurity, a great American insecurity.
> And that's what makes Steinbeck theatrical. (Smith 33)

Anderson's is a solid piece of work, and in drawing on the theme of a national insecurity that Steinbeck's dramatic works mirror, he shows what an avid amateur in Steinbeck studies can contribute while the lazy non-specialist critics sit back and admire their laurels.

Finally, there are what apparently were initial, brief presentations by DeMott, Shillinglaw, and John Seelye for a panel discussion generally entitled "John Steinbeck's Contribution to American Culture." But again, this is an occasional publication not likely obtainable through normal channels.

Robert DeMott completed his trilogy of Steinbeck titles in the same year, 1996. *Steinbeck's Typewriter* is a culling from DeMott's expansive career works on Steinbeck and his craft. Extensively illustrated and most thoroughly annotated — the bibliography even extends beyond the usual citations of first publications — DeMott's personal anthology is far more than an assemblage of nine essays, all by himself. It traces, in fact, the contour of a career in Steinbeck studies, and in itself encapsules the purpose of this present book. Thus these essays are both previously published pieces and conference papers revised, extended, and updated — and therefore also wholly new. In no sense, then, is this a self-indulgent exercise in nostalgia; it is a brightly original venture into up-to-date, fresh thought.

DeMott states that his overall purpose is "to honor Steinbeck's sense of being a self-willed writer who prized the shaping, authorizing power of imagination (however tenuous and imperfect that proved to be)," and also "to show how a welter of contextual details and intervening events gave direction to his writing life, ultimately contributing density and thickness to his published work" (DeMott, *Typewriter* xix).

For DeMott, Steinbeck is therefore "a partner in an uncertain dance" with materials, influences and sources adhering to his creative intelligence, thus making him "a negotiator of inner vision and outer resources, a mediator between internal compulsion and external forces, symbolized in the image of Steinbeck's portable typewriter . . ." (xix).

To someone who was part of DeMott's audiences when some of these essays were first delivered, the differences are plain even as the echoes are satisfying. Moreover, DeMott's scholarship and critical insight cover topics not before dealt with, such as the love poems Steinbeck wrote to the strikingly attractive singer Gwyn Conger, who became his second wife and eventually the mother of his two sons, while his first marriage to Carol Henning, who did much to help Steinbeck get his manuscripts in shape, was crumbling; or Steinbeck's indebtedness to Melville and *Moby-Dick* — not with regard to *Grapes,* as some critics have long suspected — but in terms of *East of Eden.* "*Moby-Dick* is also a testament to Quixotic obsessiveness on at least three levels" that would account for "the driven Melville's need to create a capacious fictive structure — part epic, part stage drama, part anatomy, part lyric poem — that would incorporate these antagonistic, extreme modes of perception, cognition, and being without trivializing any one of them . . ." (83).

DeMott goes on to mention that Melville's sense of the world man confronts is "mystery," and within it, Ishmael's repeated first-person statement of his need to "explain":

> . . . Steinbeck's obsessive intention in *East of Eden* was similar: he began the novel to explain the world's Manichean bipolarity and sexual mysteries to his two young sons and to introduce them to their roots via his recollection of their ancestors. (83)

DeMott has managed to parallel the classic Puritan conflict between absolutes of good and evil with the mysteries of gender that Steinbeck, like Faulkner, often seemed so baffled by. Unless they unsexed themselves, many of the women in both writers' works seem to have been at the mercy of men fixated on some absolute or other (and let's include Hawthorne as well). But by now, the male propensity for living-in-the-head has passed from the writer of *Absalom, Absalom!* to many a current woman writer (e.g., Barbara Kingsolver in *The Poisonwood Bible*).

In a chapter entitled "'One Book to a Man': Charting a Bibliographical Preface to *East of Eden*," DeMott includes a checklist of previous work on that novel. His motivation is to spur even greater critical interest in that second "big" Steinbeck novel, speaking of which Roy S. Simmonds "may have been precipitous when he predicted in his keynote address in Salinas a few years ago that the critical and scholarly 'limelight will slowly but surely shift from *The Grapes of Wrath* toward *East of Eden*'" (220), but one remembers that address as a beam of California sunlight — courtesy the United Kingdom. DeMott thinks we have a ways to go, but that "In the sense that a useful bibliography can itself be a mode of pragmatic discourse and that it too is a kind of textual negotiation — both of its subject and itself," he offers his exhaustive listing "for the last time" (221). He notes that Penguin's new editions were led off by a volume introduced by David Wyatt, that *East of Eden* was going into the Library of America series (under DeMott's direction), and adds in a parenthesis a yet-ungranted consummation devoutly to be wished:

> . . . Still needed, however, at least for serious scholars and Steinbeck aficionados, is a facsimile edition of the autograph manuscript, with its alternating sections of the daily journal and the unabridged text of the novel, or, at the very least, an edition of both novel and journal bound as one, as Steinbeck himself envisioned in 1965. (220)

One hopes that these events will happen in due time, but for the moment, DeMott (and others) have done their best to ensure that *East of Eden* eventually gets its fair hearing.

DeMott's trilogy is unique, not simply formalistically. No one else has done anything like it in terms of original coverage.

It should be obvious that the 1990s had continued the surge of strong and original critical engagements with Steinbeck's work that characterize the late 1980s. What had made the difference? It is hard not to assign a great deal of credit to Jackson Benson's biography of 1984. The second generation of Steinbeck critics was off, running, and in its sudden prime. But it is difficult to avoid the nagging suspicion that Steinbeck studies were due for redemption: for fresh and unprejudiced viewpoints; and for independent and non-defensive approaches uncowed by the blinkered bullyboys of the Eastern Establishment.

It is interesting, but not surprising, that few if any genuine Steinbeck critics come from that selfsame East, i.e., New York City, in effect; he seems to have been understood in New England and Long Island, however. Curiously, perhaps, and at the same time ironically, he has been understood terribly well by an Englishman, namely Roy S. Simmonds of Essex (see coverage of his monograph *Steinbeck's Literary Achievement* in our third chapter). His long labors produced *John Steinbeck: The War Years, 1939–1945,* in 1996. Note the years cited in his subtitle: these are the years of the War as Britons knew it, and therefore it stretches from the era of *The Grapes of Wrath* to the victories over the Axis Powers. In fact, Simmonds pursues the writing projects — some aborted, some completed — that Steinbeck had in mind during and at the end of the conflict.

Thus Simmonds takes his study up to the emergence of the 1947 titles *The Pearl* and *The Wayward Bus*. Though he has proved quite open to appreciating some of the later writings, the truncated version of his findings on *The Wayward Bus* that appears here (his longer studies of the *Bus* journals and of the text of "God in the Pipes," a fantasy — never completed — that eventually resulted in the Cannery Row novels, including *Sweet Thursday,* have not yet been allowed into print) and his coverage of *The Pearl* indicate reasons for disapproving of both, but not of the sort that would have led prior critics to assume that all thereafter was worthless.

Simmonds's ninth and final chapter is thus entitled "The Bus That Failed," but he does not have the space to make his full argument as to why that is the case. It is of considerable interest to those who have made *Bus* a special topic of study that it is one of the works which Robert DeMott and Elaine Steinbeck have seen fit to leave out of the Library of America trilogy — to date. He has, however, been carrying a rifle in hopes of bagging *The Pearl* for some time now, regarding it as a film scenario masked as a novella. In comparing the two media for which it was intended, he observes that *"The Pearl* suffers as a novella because of the cinematic point of view imposed on it, which is, here and there, intrusive" (Simmonds, *War* 258).

Simmonds knows that what works as a film scenario does not necessarily work as fiction; that "The Kino viewpoint is not, however, uniformly sustained throughout the book." He goes on to note scenic digressions as well as places where Kino's subjective mode of seeing yields to an objective one, "when the reader has been conditioned to the idea that Kino's range of vision is severely restricted" (258–59).

Simmonds's afterword ends with a section whose opening deserves quotation in a large, because thought-provoking, chunk:

> In many ways it has to be seen as regrettable that Steinbeck was not awarded the Nobel Prize in 1944 when he was first nominated and when his critical reputation was still mostly intact, for he would unquestionably have been showered with the critical accolades of his fellow-countrymen that he so richly deserved. On the other hand, one can speculate that, had he received the prize then, might it not have been the "tombstone" he had always thought of it as being? Perhaps, after all, we should be grateful to the Swedish Academy for not seeing fit to honor him then. Had they done so, the world might never have had *East of Eden,* that sprawling monolith of a novel, regarded by many as Steinbeck's best work and the one he himself always regarded, despite his reservations about it, as his "big book." (302)

Simmonds goes on to suggest increased respect for some of those other later works that are sometimes given critical short shrift: *Sweet Thursday, The Short Reign of Pippin IV, Travels With Charley,* and *The Journal of a Novel.* He reaches so far as to admire a couple of sections of *The Acts of King Arthur and His Noble Knights* (302–3).

What is going on here? Clearly, by the end of the 1990s, it was no longer necessary to kowtow to the first generation's preconceptions and misgivings; speakers in the nineties could come up with their own lists without suffering violence in the form of print retribution — or by way of simple dismissal. But for Simmonds,

> . . . Steinbeck's personal life passed through a series of crises and vicissitudes and his health was damaged, possibly even permanently, by his experiences as a war correspondent in 1943. . . .

and yet

> . . . the period 1939–45 was a period of prodigious creativity, in many
> ways matching and perhaps even exceeding the creativity of the pre-
> war years. There is no denying that Steinbeck produced an impressive
> (in volume, at least) body of work during the war years, a large por-
> tion of which is still unpublished and, for one reason or another, likely
> to remain so. This body of work, both in its published and unpub-
> lished states, has not, to date, been examined in any detail as an or-
> ganic whole. (10)

This Simmonds sets out to do, making as much reference as possible to
the unpublished writings, but not neglecting to launch forth from the
springboard of the writing of *The Grapes of Wrath*. Whatever one thinks
of the writing from the war years after reading Simmonds's remarkable
study, one has to admit to having a new vision of an output which
could have heretofore been argued to be chaotic and amorphous. Simmonds has made Steinbeck's work during the period of the war, 1939–
45 as he defines it, or 1939–47 — a period itself chaotic and therefore
arguably amorphous — seem rather more like a pattern the lineaments
of which have yet to be clearly perceived. In so doing, he goes well beyond whatever fleshing-out of Benson's account of the 1940s Parini
may have accomplished. Like luggage in an overhead compartment, the
weight of critical attention was surely shifting towards the later works in
the 1990s.

In 1997, Viking Press published the result of its approach to Peter
Lisca to revise the contents of its 1972 critical edition of *The Grapes of
Wrath* in order to reflect the changes in critical directions of a quarter-
century, and also to take advantage of the recently-restored text of the
novel already published in the Library of America series. (Thus the text
is preceded by a list of corrections and restorations keyed to the present
volume.) Eventually Lisca, by then preoccupied with other concerns,
chose as editorial colleague Kevin Hearle, by then an independent
scholar whose work has already been mentioned in these pages.

The results are naturally of interest to anyone familiar with the previous volume. "*The Grapes of Wrath*": *Text and Criticism* includes a
map, three classic essays on the novel's social context (as if to bow in
that once automatic direction), and then a section on "The Creative
Context," including reprinted pieces by Benson and DeMott, and
Steinbeck's own "suggestions" for an interview with Joseph Henry
Jackson in the wake of the novel's initial heady release.

The "Criticism" section is the volume's richest, and yet it also suc-
cumbs to the tendency to include safe and standby, previously printed

pieces. But these are usually of unquestionable value. Nellie Y. McKay's contribution comes from the aforementioned David Wyatt anthology, but its observations about Ma Joad are worth repeating here:

> But although the structure of the traditional family changes to meet the needs of a changing society, in this novel at least Steinbeck sees "happy-wife-and-motherdom" as the central role for women, even for with other central contributions to make to the world at large. Ma Joad's education in the possibilities of class action do not extend to an awareness of women's lives and identities beyond the domestic sphere, other than that which has a direct relationship to the survival of the family. (Lisca/Hearle 680)

Kevin Hearle's considerable work on this revisionist edition of *The Grapes of Wrath* will pay off for decades to come for a generation of student readers.

Interestingly, it is only before the book's fourth section, "Criticism," that the editors place their joint introduction. The reasons seem patent enough quickly enough: Lisca and Hearle know that this edition, beyond its textual emendations, will be of primary interest for its ability to transcend eras and register trends, and it is to that end, perhaps, that they come down on the side of one of the latter, and heavily, if only for pragmatic reasons: "Although all of these newer schools . . . have made solid contributions to Steinbeck criticism, the new approach which arguably has been most influential in Steinbeck studies to date has been feminism" (Lisca & Hearle 560). True enough, perhaps, nor does this preclude inclusion of such by-now-classic essays as John R. Reed's on "The Esthetics of Indigence"; on the other hand, in spite of the inclusion of the customary discussion questions, this text seems meant for almost unusually perceptive undergraduates as well as graduate students, and it is certainly this writer's experience that the latter, at least, approach Steinbeck (and other authors) with an intimidating amount of feminist critical theory, a fact of university life in the late 1990s that is hardly at all reflected here.

All in all, though, *"The Grapes of Wrath": Text and Criticism* is a most useful collection of materials, particularly when constructively compared to its predecessor — with a price that makes it student-attainable, even if its reliance on so much recent matter available in fuller format elsewhere makes it a dubious shelf addition for any specialists who are not also collectors. (Interestingly if finally perhaps irrelevantly enough — or perhaps not — a high percentage of Steinbeckians are also bibliophiles.) At any rate, one can count on this volume's availability for some time to come, more so than on its paper stock to last.

As Brian Railsback has been memorably quoted above as recalling, the Nantucket Conference on Steinbeck and the Environment of 1992 was something of a magical experience. *Steinbeck and the Environment: Interdisciplinary Approaches* may give the secret away with its subtitle; for a change, the embattled Steinbeckians, used to listening to the dull roar of out-of-touch celebrity speakers, instead got to mingle with scientists, social philosophers, and of course environmentalists — their profession having come of age during Steinbeck's lifetime and especially thereafter. Persons who thought that for years they had been addressing the proverbial brick wall found that all the while, and just behind them, were numbers of individuals from seemingly disparate disciplines who had understood all along what the stakes had been, and moreover, had been reading and — yes! — understanding Steinbeck as a vital component of their own commitment. Sudden alliances can be as empowering as fresh air can be invigorating.

Not all the papers presented made it into this fine collection, and considerable editorial work was required before the results were issued five years later. The three editors were Susan Shillinglaw; Susan Beegel, then affiliated with the University of Idaho; and her husband Wesley N. Tiffney, Jr., director of the Nantucket Field Station of the University of Massachusetts — to speak of which venue is to remember scholars dining on box lunches on a grassy cliff facing towards Portugal, Elaine Steinbeck in attendance, or collecting scallop shells below. This trio epitomizes what went on there and then.

The contents are unprecedented in their variety, and in the degree in which they evidence the great interest of many Steinbeckians in matters scientific or at least environmental — as well as, perhaps surprising to the critics, the ways in which a parallel universe of interest in Steinbeck was suddenly seen to have existed, unsuspected — like some heretofore undiscovered galaxy.

Not surprisingly, two of these five well-balanced sections of this commemorative anthology deal with *The Grapes of Wrath* and *Sea of Cortez*, the latter just past its fiftieth anniversary of publication. (It is on *Sea* that Stanley Brodwin delivered his unforgettably brilliant seeming-improvisation, here in a more conventionalized format.) A first section deals, in two essays, with the origins of Steinbeck's (and Ricketts's) thinking. A fourth contains essays on the later works, with such names as John Burroughs and Herman Melville suggesting the multidisciplinary field being established (this time, DeMott does indeed get to

Moby-Dick). Finally, a fifth section assesses Steinbeck's work and thought in terms of what must be called its timeliness, or its ability to fit within the ecological concerns of a supposedly more committed era, one in which scientific objectivity has been largely replaced by an ethical anxiety over the future of the planet.

To which purpose editor Tiffney, in the first part of the book's triune introduction, notes that "Neither Ricketts nor Steinbeck would be regarded as an environmental scientist today . . . Rather both men were advanced early ecologists, not only evaluating organisms in relation to the physical environment, but also considering living populations, including man, in relation to each other" (Beegel 4). Tiffney goes on to say to the reader of the present time tempted to judge these men by convenient hindsight that "if some of their ideas and philosophy seem a little naive and self-evident, or their marine collecting practices seem 'environmentally incorrect' to us today, remember that fifty-five years have passed since *Sea of Cortez* saw print, and our ideas and approaches have changed. Ricketts and Steinbeck were pioneer ecological thinkers and we should not chastise them for lacking the benefit of our 'modern' and 'enlightened' ideas" (4–5).

Tiffney's conclusion encapsules what drew scientists and literary critics together on this occasion:

> Steinbeck and Ricketts's outstanding idea is that microcosm and macrocosm are interacting entities and part of a grand, interlaced continuum embracing human society. Within this continuum, no part can do without the whole. As the essays in this volume demonstrate, literature and literary critics are not isolated from the ideas and products of science, and scientists do not live apart from the concepts and reality of literature. Here, both are parts of the intellectual whole. (7)

Susan Shillinglaw's perspective (as these introductions are called) comes next, and while its approach is by way of the historical recital of events, she concisely names the compounds that went into the alembic of the formative years of Steinbeck's philosophy of science: "The year 1932 was, I believe, the generative time, perhaps the annus mirabilis for Ricketts's lab circle. That year Joseph Campbell lived briefly in Pacific Grove" (10–11). And so on, citing all that caused such a heady ferment. She pays tribute to the included essays because they "fill gaps in our appreciation of Steinbeck's approach to 'the problem,' a holistic appreciation of life" (13).

Susan Beegel writes as a "generalist," and her approach is largely if also modestly autobiographical. Having read some but not by any means all of Steinbeck, she recalls,

I encountered a corrective sneer in Wes Tiffney's lab. Somehow, upon my wandering in to pass the time of day with the various scientists at work there, Wes forced me to confess aloud that I had never read *Log from the Sea of Cortez* or *Cannery Row,* and well do I remember the shattering silence that greeted this announcement. (14)

The message was clear: not only did scientists take it for granted that their peers would know Steinbeck, but they at least feigned astonishment that a serious teacher of literature might not have. Beegel has wonderfully recovered:

Novel as ecology, setting as habitat, characters as fauna, cooperation as redemption — the understanding of the environment that pervades Steinbeck's work results from a profoundly interdisciplinary habit of mind and a uniquely interdisciplinary friendship. If Steinbeck was a novelist who thought as an ecologist, . . . Ed Ricketts . . . was a marine biologist who thought as a philosopher. Science and the humanities are not compartmentalized in their minds. (19)

As noted above, there was no precedent for this invaluable volume; but it seems safe to conclude that it will have its share of successors as Steinbeck specialists, always aware to the point of near-embarrassment of the breadth of their subject's audience, realize more and more that they had not perceived "the half of it."

Steinbeck and the Environment is the last of the titles to be surveyed in this fifth chapter. With it, we are just about up to date and ready to turn to some tentative efforts towards a conclusion. It was noted earlier that Steinbeck had a fear that he would die young. To those approaching his age at death — 66 — or already past it, it might very much seem that it was so, as Steinbeck might have put it. At least this much is certain from our survey of the book-length studies of Steinbeck published during the 1990s: the age of minimal generalist treatments of the man and his work is over, and from now on Steinbeck scholarship is going to move in all possible directions outward, though without, one suspects, its participants ever losing full contact with one another.

Works Consulted

Beegel, Susan F., Susan Shillinglaw, and Wesley N. Tiffney, Jr., eds. *Steinbeck and the Environment: Interdisciplinary Approaches*. Tuscaloosa: U Alabama P, 1997.

Benson, Jackson J., ed. *The Short Novels of John Steinbeck: Critical Essays with a Checklist to Steinbeck Criticism*. Durham, NC: Duke U P, 1990.

Coers, Donald V. *John Steinbeck as Propagandist: "The Moon Is Down" Goes to War*. Tuscaloosa: U Alabama P, 1991.

———, Paul D. Ruffin, and Robert J. DeMott, eds. *After "The Grapes of Wrath": Essays on John Steinbeck in Honor of Tetsumaro Hayashi*. Athens: Ohio U P, 1995.

DeMott, Robert. *Steinbeck's Typewriter: Essays on His Art*. Troy, NY: Whitston Publishing, 1996.

Enea, Sparky, as told to Audry Lynch. *With Steinbeck in the Sea of Cortez*. Los Osos, CA: Sand River P, 1991.

French, Warren. *John Steinbeck's Fiction Revisited*. New York: Twayne, 1994.

———. *John Steinbeck's Nonfiction Revisited*. New York: Twayne, 1996.

Galati, Frank, adaptor. *"The Grapes of Wrath."* London: Warner Chappell Plays, 1991.

Hadella, Charlotte Cook. *"Of Mice and Men": A Kinship of Powerlessness*. New York: Twayne, 1995.

Lisca, Peter, and Kevin Hearle, eds. *"The Grapes of Wrath": Text and Criticism*. New York: Penguin Books, 1997.

Noble, Donald R., ed. *The Steinbeck Question: New Essays in Criticism*. Troy, NY: Whitston Publishing, 1993.

Parini, Jay. *John Steinbeck: A Biography*. New York: Henry Holt, 1995.

Railsback, Brian E. *Parallel Expeditions: Charles Darwin and the Art of John Steinbeck*. Moscow, ID: U Idaho P, 1995.

Simmonds, Roy. *John Steinbeck: The War Years, 1939–1945*. Lewisburg, PA: Bucknell U P, 1996.

Smith, Joel A., ed. *Steinbeck: On Stage & Film*. Louisville, KY: Actors Theatre of Louisville, 1996.

Timmerman, John H. *The Dramatic Landscape of John Steinbeck's Short Stories*. Norman: U Oklahoma P, 1990.

Wyatt, David, ed. *New Essays on "The Grapes of Wrath."* New York: Cambridge U P, 1990.

6: Conclusions

IT IS TIME TO TRACE THE TRAJECTORY of Steinbeck studies over the last sixty years — at least so far as book-length criticism is concerned. And yet the term "trajectory" itself smacks of lobbed missiles, of things thrown high that descend again to earth. Steinbeck studies show no sign of such diminishment — let alone crashing.

Rather, the books surveyed here suggest an upward curve in little danger of collapsing — more like the Dow Jones index of the 1990s, viewed year to year, than any standard American literary career's progress.

The writing about Steinbeck in the 1940s and 1950s shows a dutiful concern with maintenance; after all, the writer was still alive and there was no telling what he might try next. The surveys of this period are apt to be doggedly chronological and dependent for philosophical and critical insights on what Steinbeck and Ricketts left behind as clues, that is, on what they said they were all about.

By the time of Steinbeck's death in late 1968, it had become clear that nothing more — or precious little — was going to come from that original source. Critics continued to mine some of the same materials, but now covering the final writings as well. Critics began to address biographical concerns, and as if anticipating Steinbeck as the marketable commodity he is today, they gave increased attention to *place* as a valid focus of attention, if only in terms of the early writing. It was also becoming less and less important to find a salient on which to declare one's partial critical independence. Steinbeck's influence as a media presence began to receive first focus.

As noted above, and repeatedly, the 1950s and 1960s were a time of series-title projects, with the inherent limitations of books meant primarily for automatic library sales. All academic presses seemed to want to have their own horse running in the Steinbeck derby. Curiously, however, this was also a time in which two contradictory situations came into existence simultaneously and, perhaps, unprecedentedly: Steinbeck titles remained in widespread print and his readership was seemingly undiminished; and yet his critical reputation continued towards its nadir, as if his critics were almost wholly out of touch with the clientele they were supposedly meant to serve.

The results of this situation have asserted themselves in what may be unique ways over the years since Steinbeck's death. While it is true that fewer books have been devoted to Steinbeck's writings than to Faulkner, Hemingway, or Melville, for example — as observed earlier — one does not yet have to be an idiot savant to master all of it. This is a saving grace for the right graduate student.

One cannot overemphasize the significance of the Steinbeck Society and its leader, Tetsumaro Hayashi, over a period that includes parts or all of three decades. Ted Hayashi and his cohorts gave Steinbeck studies an extra lift when one was most needed. It is not the case that all of the important papers and books after the late 1960s were published under the auspices of the Steinbeck Society; but many if not most of them were. Hayashi simply carried on as though an implacable critical enemy did not exist; and in the end, his instincts proved him right. Moreover, many a scholar — whether or not a member of the Society — owes a debt of gratitude to Hayashi's incredible energies. And it would be remiss to ignore the help his bibliographies, however sometimes flawed they might have been in terms of redundancies and other citational errors, have been to students at all levels. In short, had Ted Hayashi not existed one would have had to find a way to invent him — but without success!

By no means were the 1980s exclusively the decade of "revisions," anymore that the 1990s were on of the "visions," yet the rubric still holds overall. As our fourth chapter demonstrates, a number of Steinbeck's first serious critics saw fit to make thoughtful reconsiderations of their stances in the eighties. The era produced the "definitive" Steinbeck biography at Jack Benson's hands. Studies of the short stories and of dramatizations of Steinbeck's work were afoot. In spite of continuing dismissals by the patently ignorant, Steinbeck's writings had become a permanently valid focus of critical inquiry.

The late 1980s and early 1990s saw the arrival of sustained studies of Steinbeck's short fiction. Reminiscences and focuses on place declined in number, and for obvious reasons. Another strong biography appeared, and towards the end of the decade, a number of extraordinarily important studies and anthologies were published, perhaps signaling a transitional period in which the second generation of Steinbeck critics were making their final, or at least penultimate, statements, and also ceding turf to newer speakers and newer voices. No longer constrained by the prejudices the second generation grew up under during its university days, the newcomers clearly felt free to run off coolly in all directions.

Specialized studies during the past two decades were not at all narrowly devoted to special pleading(s). At a time when Steinbeck entries, such as the once-routine "Flight" and "The Chrysanthemums," began to disappear from university anthologies, these classics of American short fiction went on being read in spite of the apparent and appalling ignorance (or plain fecklessness) of editors. It would appear that not only had the Arthur Mizeners and Edmund Wilsons and Harold Blooms and Leslie Fiedlers of the world spoken out of due course and season, but that their lock-step followers were as much as half a century out of synch.

As noted at our beginning of this survey, there are materials that could not be included under the realistic rubric of books about Steinbeck's books. Thus films made from Steinbeck's works have been largely unattended to — such as certain recent adaptations of stories, Hollywood's versions of certain novels, television adaptations of other works (such as Robert Blake's reconstruction of Lewis Milestone's *Of Mice and Men* or the recent cable biography of Steinbeck, which features some of the personalities by now familiar to our readers — Benson, Shillinglaw, Parini, and Elaine Steinbeck), operatic treatments, and even stage adaptations (unless accompanied by a written critical text). These have all possessed valid interpretive value; but our business has had to do with books.

However, the print medium did contribute two items of public interest at the end of the 1990s. First of all, and most notoriously, there was issued a 1998 listing of the so-called hundred most important novels of the century, under Random House's Modern Library auspices. Naturally, there was an immediate fuss about inclusions and exclusions; and some of the panelists (and a very small panel it was, indeed) later expressed themselves in print about their deliberations in ways that suggest bafflement at what they had wrought and how they had wrought it. In the end, what they could agree to include consisted mainly of what most of them had read long ago — and that allowed for the ready inclusion of John Steinbeck in their final list. Indeed, *The Grapes of Wrath* was tenth.

Furthermore, Robert DeMott (in a letter) has reminded me of two other, and far more inclusive, polls recently conducted. *Hungry Mind Review*, based in Minneapolis, conducted its own listing of the best American prose of the Twentieth Century early in 1999. *The Grapes of Wrath* won a place among the chosen few.

DeMott also reports that slightly later, Paul Lauter's *The Heath Anthology of American Literature Newsletter* conducted its own poll, and here again *The Grapes of Wrath* scored high — seventh place out of the top nine. It would seem that whether the voters are exclusivist or "inclusivist," Steinbeck is aboard unless some patent bias has been at work.

Later in 1999, Houghton Mifflin published *The Best American Short Stories of the Century*, supposedly the "best of the best" from the long-running *Best American Short Stories* annual; from decades of material editorial assistant Katrina Kenison chose a couple of hundred titles from which John Updike made the final cut. Though he is mentioned in the foreword, John Steinbeck does not appear among the writers of the "best" — and so the writer of *The Long Valley* stories ends up with no place at the table for this putative feast.

There is no point in arguing about anthologies, but two points can readily be made about this one. First, it reflects the sort of cultural-studies biases that have been the curse (and the source of curses) for many literature teachers in the recent age of political correctness; the idea is to include as many minorities as possible, not primarily to pick the "best of the best." Secondly, the critical juggernaut created by persons who perhaps have not read Steinbeck and dismiss those who do is still out there, rolling along mindlessly.

Thus we are left observing that incremental upward curve, one that shows little sign of leveling off very soon. While, as Mimi Gladstein observed earlier on, the field of Steinbeck studies is not nearly as overcrowded as those for, say, Hemingway and Faulkner, it is also still possible for a newcomer to the field to get some grasp of all the important Steinbeck criticism to date, and then to carve a new and individual niche in it. A teacher of, for example, a Steinbeck seminar at the Master's level at the present day would likely encounter a dual but not contradictory phenomenon: students open to Steinbeck but largely previously ignorant of him — and yet apt to find him of their time, refreshingly "there" in their presences and most clearly audible; and the same students able to bring to their first extended readings of Steinbeck their own backgrounds in critical theory (often intimidating to their own professors) and such trendy, but ultimately Steinbeck-friendly, fields as cultural studies.

I often think, on driving from my home in Detroit south (a geographical anomaly) to Windsor, Ontario, of the implications of crossing an international border every workday. This is especially true when the matter for the day is Steinbeck, for over the years my students (often previously only exposed to some basic Steinbeck materials in high school, such as *The Red Pony* or *Of Mice and Men*) find themselves at ease with the rest of his writings and have responded well to Steinbeck, and a number of my graduate seminar papers on him have been published. (Indeed, the late celebrated Canadian author W. O. Mitchell once confessed to me Steinbeck's influence on his work.) If this seems unremarkable among Canadians, surely it is remarkable when one considers his European and Asiatic readership, especially Japanese. There is obviously a universality about Steinbeck that speaks to people the world over. His books have sold well, and stayed in print, for well over sixty years. To some, sales and popularity are a red flag signaling a lack of literary value; but would that apply to a *Cold Mountain* or to *Angela's Ashes?* But even these books are dwarfed in ongoing popularity by Steinbeck's. And to some critics, popularity as reflected in sales is the unforgivable sin.

Compared to America's — and the world's — other losses in 1968, the death of John Steinbeck might have been seen as a mere blip on the year's telescreen. And yet the *Steinbeck Quarterly* was able to begin publication in the year of Steinbeck's death and make consistent and sustained contributions to a corpus in need of sustenance. Thereafter Steinbeck studies were off and running.

Sixty years of books on John Steinbeck's writings have done their work.

There is no need to look back anymore.

A Chronological Listing of Works Cited

1939

Gannett, Lewis. *John Steinbeck: Personal and Bibliographical Notes.* New York: Viking.

Moore, Harry Thornton. *The Novels of John Steinbeck: A First Study.* Chicago: Normandie House.

1946

Gannett, Lewis, ed. *The Portable Steinbeck.* New York: Viking.

1957

Tedlock, E. W., Jr., and C. V. Wicker, eds. *Steinbeck and His Critics.* Albuquerque: U New Mexico P.

1958

Lisca, Peter. *The Wide World of John Steinbeck.* New Brunswick, NJ: Rutgers UP.

1961

French, Warren, ed. *John Steinbeck.* New York: Twayne.

1962

Watt, F. W. *John Steinbeck.* New York: Grove.

1963

Fontenrose, Joseph. *John Steinbeck: An Introduction and Interpretation.* New York: Holt, Rinehart and Winston.

French, Warren, ed. *A Companion to "The Grapes of Wrath."* New York: Viking.

1967

Gale, Robert L. *Barron's Simplified Approach to Steinbeck: "Grapes of Wrath."* Woodbury, NY: Barron's.

1968

Donohue, Agnes McNeill. *A Casebook on "The Grapes of Wrath."* New York: Crowell.

1969

Marks, Lester Jay. *Thematic Design in the Novels of John Steinbeck.* The Hague: Mouton.

1970

O'Connor, Richard. *John Steinbeck.* New York: McGraw-Hill.

Pratt, John Clark. *John Steinbeck.* Grand Rapids, MI: Eerdmans.

1971

Astro, Richard, and Tetsumaro Hayashi, eds. *Steinbeck: The Man and His Work.* Corvallis: Oregon State UP.

Burrows, Michael. *John Steinbeck and His Films.* St. Austell, UK: Primestyle.

Covici, Pascal, ed. *The Portable Steinbeck.* New York: Viking.

Gray, James. *John Steinbeck.* Minneapolis: U Minnesota P.

Hayashi, Tetsumaro, ed. *John Steinbeck: A Guide to the Doctoral Dissertations.* Muncie, IN: Steinbeck Monograph Series No. 1.

1972

Davis, Robert Murray, ed. *Steinbeck: A Collection of Critical Essays.* Englewood Cliffs, NJ: Prentice-Hall.

Garcia, Reloy. *Steinbeck and D. H. Lawrence: Fictive Voices and the Ethical Imperative.* Muncie, IN: Steinbeck Monograph Series No. 2.

Lisca, Peter, ed. *John Steinbeck: "The Grapes of Wrath": Text and Criticism.* New York: Viking.

1973

Astro, Richard. *John Steinbeck and Edward F. Ricketts: The Shaping of a Novelist.* Minneapolis: U Minnesota P.

Crouch, Steve. *Steinbeck Country.* Palo Alto, CA: American West.

French, Warren. *Filmguide to "The Grapes of Wrath"* Bloomington: Indiana U P.

Hayashi, Tetsumaro. *A New Steinbeck Bibliography, 1929–1971.* Metuchen, NJ: Scarecrow.

Jones, Lawrence William, ed. Marston LaFrance. *John Steinbeck as Fabulist.* Muncie, IN: Steinbeck Monograph Series No. 3.

1974

Hayashi, Tetsumaro, ed. *Steinbeck Criticism: A Review of Book-Length Studies (1939–1973)*. Muncie, IN: Steinbeck Monograph Series No. 4.

————, ed. *A Study Guidebook to Steinbeck: A Handbook to His Major Works*. Metuchen, NJ: Scarecrow.

Levant, Howard. *The Novels of John Steinbeck: A Critical Study*. Columbia: U Missouri.

1975

Astro, Richard, and Joel W. Hedgpeth, eds. *Steinbeck and the Sea*. Corvallis: Oregon State UP.

French, Warren. *John Steinbeck*, rev. ed. Boston: Twayne.

Hayashi, Tetsumaro, ed. *Steinbeck and the Arthurian Theme*. Muncie, IN: Steinbeck Monograph Series No. 5.

Valjean, Nelson. *John Steinbeck: The Errant Knight*. San Francisco: Chronicle.

1976

Astro, Richard. *Edward F. Ricketts*. Boise: Boise State U.

Hayashi, Tetsumaro, ed. *A Study Guide to Steinbeck's "The Long Valley."* Ann Arbor, MI: Pierian.

———— and Kenneth D. Swan, eds. *Steinbeck's Prophetic Vision of America*. Upland, IN: Taylor U P.

Simmonds, Roy S. *Steinbeck's Literary Achievement*. Muncie, IN: Steinbeck Monograph Series No. 6.

1977

Ditsky, John. *Essays on "East of Eden."* Muncie, IN: Steinbeck Monograph Series No. 7.

1978

Hayashi, Tetsumaro, Yasuo Hashiguchi, and Richard F. Peterson, eds. *John Steinbeck: East and West* Muncie, IN: Steinbeck Monograph Series No. 8.

Hedgpeth, Joel W., ed. *The Outer Shores,* Part One. Eureka, CA: Mad River Press.

Lisca, Peter. *John Steinbeck: Nature and Myth*. New York: Crowell.

Schmitz, Anne-Marie. *In Search of Steinbeck*. Los Altos, CA: Hermes.

1979

Fensch, Thomas. *Steinbeck and Covici: The Story of a Friendship.* Middlebury, VT: Eriksson.

Hayashi, Tetsumaro, ed. *Steinbeck's Women: Essays in Criticism.* Muncie, IN: Steinbeck Monograph Series No. 9.

———, ed. *A Study Guidebook to Steinbeck (Part II).* Metuchen, NJ: Scarecrow.

Hedgpeth, Joel W., ed. *The Outer Shores,* Part Two. Eureka, CA: Mad River Press.

Kiernan, Thomas. *The Intricate Music: A Biography of John Steinbeck.* Boston: Little, Brown.

1980

Hayashi, Tetsumaro, ed. *Steinbeck and Hemingway: Dissertation Abstracts and Research Opportunities.* Metuchen , NJ: Scarecrow.

———, ed. *Steinbeck's Travel Literature: Essays in Criticism* Muncie, IN: Steinbeck Monograph Series No. 10.

McCarthy, Paul. *John Steinbeck.* New York: Ungar.

1981

Fontenrose, Joseph. *Steinbeck's Unhappy Valley.* Berkeley, CA: Joseph Fontenrose.

Hayashi, Tetsumaro., ed. *A Handbook for Steinbeck Collectors, Librarians, and Scholars.* Muncie, IN: Steinbeck Monograph Series No. 11.

1982

Davis, Robert Con, ed. *Twentieth Century Interpretations of "The Grapes of Wrath."* Englewood Cliffs, NJ: Prentice-Hall.

1983

Martin, Stoddard. *California Writers: Jack London, John Steinbeck, The Tough Guys.* New York: St. Martin's P.

Millichap, Joseph R. *Steinbeck and Film:* New York: Ungar.

St. Pierre, Brian. *John Steinbeck: The California Years.* San Francisco: Chronicle.

Weber, Tom. *Cannery Row: A Time to Remember.* Monterey, CA: Orenda/Unity.

Hayashi, Tetsumaro, *A New Steinbeck Bibliography, 1971–1981.* Metuchen, NJ: Scarecrow.

1984

Benson, Jackson. *The True Adventures of John Steinbeck, Writer.* New York: Viking.

DeMott, Robert. *Steinbeck's Reading: A Catalogue of Books Owned and Borrowed.* New York: Garland.

1985

Owens, Louis *John Steinbeck's Re-Vision of America.* Athens: U Georgia P.

1986

Gladstein, Mimi R. *The Indestructible Woman in Faulkner, Hemingway, and Steinbeck.* Ann Arbor, MI: UMI Research Press.

Hayashi, Tetsumaro. *John Steinbeck and the Vietnam War (Part I).* Muncie, IN: Steinbeck Monograph Series No. 12.

————, *Steinbeck's World War II Fiction, "The Moon Is Down": Three Explications.* Muncie, IN: Steinbeck Essay Series No. 1.

————, *A Student's Guide to Steinbeck's Literature: Primary and Secondary Sources.* Muncie, IN: Steinbeck Bibliography Series No. 1.

Timmerman, John H. *John Steinbeck's Fiction: The Aesthetics of the Road Taken.* Norman: U Oklahoma P.

1987

Bloom, Harold, ed. *John Steinbeck.* New York: Chelsea House.

Hughes, R. S. *Beyond The Red Pony: A Reader's Companion to Steinbeck's Complete Short Stories.* Metuchen, NJ: Scarecrow.

1988

Benson, Jackson J. *Looking for Steinbeck's Ghost.* Norman: U Oklahoma P.

Bloom, Harold, ed. *John Steinbeck's "The Grapes of Wrath."* New York: Chelsea House.

Fensch, Thomas, ed. *Conversations with John Steinbeck.* Jackson: U P of Mississippi.

Hayashi, Tetsumaro, ed. *John Steinbeck on Writing.* Muncie, IN: Steinbeck Essay Series No. 2.

———— and Thomas J. Moore, eds. *Steinbeck's "The Red Pony": Essays in Criticism.* Muncie, IN: Steinbeck Monograph Series No. 13.

Whitebrook, Peter. *Staging Steinbeck: Dramatising "The Grapes of Wrath."* London: Cassell.

1989

DeMott, Robert, ed. *Working Days: The Journals of "The Grapes of Wrath."* New York: Viking.

Ditsky, John, ed. *Critical Essays on Steinbeck's "The Grapes of Wrath."* Boston: G. K. Hall.

Hayashi, Tetsumaro, and Thomas J. Moore, eds. *Steinbeck's Posthumous Work: Essays in Criticism.* Muncie, IN: Steinbeck Monograph Series No. 14.

Hughes, R. S. *John Steinbeck: A Study of the Short Fiction.* Boston: Twayne.

Lewis, Cliff, and Carroll Britch, eds. *Rediscovering Steinbeck: Revisionist Views of His Art, Politics and Intellect.* Lewiston, NY: Edwin Mellen P.

Owens, Louis. *"The Grapes of Wrath": Trouble in the Promised Land.* Boston: Twayne.

1990

Benson, Jackson J., ed. The Short Novels of John Steinbeck*: Critical Essays with a Checklist to Steinbeck Criticism.* Durham, NC: Duke U P.

Hayashi, Tetsumaro, ed. *Steinbeck's "The Grapes of Wrath": Essays in Criticism.* Muncie, IN: Steinbeck Essay Series No. 3.

Timmerman, John H. *The Dramatic Landscape of John Steinbeck's Short Stories.* Norman: U Oklahoma P.

Wyatt, David, ed. *New Essays on "The Grapes of Wrath."* New York: Cambridge U P.

1991

Benson, Jackson J. *Steinbeck's "Cannery Row": A Reconsideration.* Muncie, IN: Steinbeck Essay Series No. 4.

Coers, Donald V. *John Steinbeck as Propagandist: "The Moon Is Down" Goes to War.* Tuscaloosa: U Alabama P.

Enea, Sparky, as told to Audry Lynch. *With Steinbeck in the Sea of Cortez.* Los Osos, CA: Sand River P.

Galati, Frank, adaptor. *"The Grapes of Wrath."* London: Warner Chappell Plays.

Hayashi, Tetsumaro, ed. *Steinbeck's Literary Dimension: A Guide to Comparative Studies.* Metuchen, NJ: Scarecrow.

———, ed. *Steinbeck's Short Stories in "The Long Valley": Essays in Criticism.* Muncie, IN: Steinbeck Monograph Series No. 15.

1993

Hayashi, Tetsumaro, ed. *John Steinbeck: The Years of Greatness, 1936–1939*. Tuscaloosa. U Alabama P.

———, ed. *A New Study Guide to Steinbeck's Major Works, with Critical Explications*. Metuchen, NJ: Scarecrow.

Noble, Donald R., ed. *The Steinbeck Question: New Essays in Criticism*. Troy, NY: Whitston Publishing.

1994

French, Warren. *John Steinbeck's Fiction Revisited*. New York: Twayne.

1995

Coers, Donald V., Paul D. Ruffin, and Robert J. DeMott, eds. *After "The Grapes of Wrath": Essays on John Steinbeck in Honor of Tetsumaro Hayashi*. Athens: Ohio U P.

Hadella, Charlotte Cook. *"Of Mice and Men": A Kinship of Powerlessness*. New York: Twayne.

Parini, Jay. *John Steinbeck: A Biography*. New York: Henry Holt.

Railsback, Brian E. *Parallel Expeditions: Charles Darwin and the Art of John Steinbeck*. Moscow, ID: U Idaho P.

1996

DeMott, Robert. *Steinbeck's Typewriter: Essays on His Art*. Troy, NY: Whitston Publishing.

French, Warren. *John Steinbeck's Nonfiction Revisited*. New York: Twayne.

Simmonds, Roy. *John Steinbeck: The War Years, 1939–1945*. Lewisburg, PA: Bucknell U P.

Smith, Joel A., ed. *Steinbeck: On Stage & Film*. Louisville, KY: Actors Theatre of Louisville.

1997

Beegel, Susan F., Susan Shillinglaw, and Wesley N. Tiffney, Jr., eds. *Steinbeck and the Environment: Interdisciplinary Approaches*. Tuscaloosa: U Alabama P.

Lisca, Peter, and Kevin Hearle, eds. *"The Grapes of Wrath": Text and Criticism*. New York: Penguin.

1998

Meyer, Michael, ed. *The Hayashi Steinbeck Bibliography, 1982–1996*. Lanham, MD: Scarecrow.

A Chronological Listing of Works by John Steinbeck

(First Publications)

1929

Cup of Gold. New York: Robert M. McBride.

1932

The Pastures of Heaven. New York: Brewer, Warren and Putnam.

1933

To a God Unknown. New York: Robert A. Ballou.

1935

Tortilla Flat. New York: Covici-Friede.

1936

In Dubious Battle. New York: Covici-Friede.

1937

Of Mice and Men (novel). New York: Covici-Friede.
Of Mice and Men (play). New York: Covici-Friede.
The Red Pony. New York: Covici-Friede.

1938

Their Blood Is Strong (journalism). San Francisco: Samuel J. Lubin Society.
The Long Valley. New York: Viking.

1939

The Grapes of Wrath. New York: Viking.

1941

Sea of Cortez: A Leisurely Journal of Travel and Research. New York: Viking.
The Forgotten Village (film script). New York: Viking.

1942

Bombs Away: The Story of a Bomber Team (journalism). New York: Viking.

The Moon Is Down (novel). New York: Viking.

The Moon Is Down (play). New York: Dramatists' Play Service.

1945

Cannery Row. New York: Viking.

1947

The Wayward Bus. New York: Viking.

The Pearl. New York: Viking.

1948

A Russian Journal (journalism). New York: Viking.

1950

Burning Bright (novel). New York: Viking.

1951

Burning Bright (play). New York: Dramatists' Play Service.

The Log from the "Sea of Cortez" (narrative portion plus memoir, "About Ed Ricketts"). New York: Viking.

1952

East of Eden. New York: Viking.

1954

Sweet Thursday. New York: Viking.

1957

The Short Reign of Pippin IV: A Fabrication. New York: Viking.

1958

Once There Was a War (journalism). New York: Viking.

1961

The Winter of Our Discontent. New York: Viking.

1962

Speech Accepting the Nobel Prize for Literature. New York: Viking.

Travels with Charley in Search of America (journalism). New York: Viking.

1966

America and Americans (journalism). New York: Viking.

1969

Journal of a Novel: The "East of Eden" Letters. New York: Viking.

1975

Viva Zapata! (film script), ed. Robert E. Morsberger. New York: Viking.

Steinbeck: A Life in Letters, ed. Elaine Steinbeck and Robert Wallsten. New York: Viking.

1976

The Acts of King Arthur and His Noble Knights, ed. Chase Horton. New York: Farrar, Straus & Giroux.

1978

Letters to Elizabeth: A Selection of Letters from John Steinbeck to Elizabeth Otis, ed. Florian J. Shasky and Susan F. Riggs. San Francisco: Book Club of California.

1979

Steinbeck and Covici: The Story of a Friendship, ed. Thomas Fensch. Middlebury, VT: Paul S. Eriksson.

1981

Selected Essays of John Steinbeck, ed. Hidekazu Hirose and Kiyoshi Nakayama. Tokyo: Shinozake Shorin P.

1986

Uncollected Stories of John Steinbeck, ed. Kiyoshi Nakayama. Tokyo: Nan'un Do.

1988

Working Days: The Journal of "The Grapes of Wrath," ed. Robert DeMott. New York: Viking.

1991

Zapata (scenario, introduction, and film script). London: Heinemann.

Index